RABBITLOPAEDIA

A Complete Guide To Rabbit Care

D0333040

*Meg Brown and
Virginia Richardson
MA Vet MB MRCVS*

RINGPRESS

ACKNOWLEDGEMENTS

I thank all my friends at home and abroad for their help and encouragement in putting this book together. In particular I would like to thank Dr Tom Coateam of Pennsylvania for his assistance on things American, and my nieces, Fiona Mackie and Sheena Lomas, for sketches and plant paintings. Above all, however, I am most indebted to Mrs Kinns – our librarian – for all the help she has given me unstintingly over the last year. She checked each page for me, making suggestions and digging out information, even though some of the things I asked her about caused her to use quite a lot of her own time in researching. She is the pillar on which this book stands and I am most grateful indeed.

Meg Brown

Published by INTERPET PUBLISHING
Vincent Lane, Dorking, Surrey, RH4 3YX

© 2000 RINGPRESS BOOKS
REPRINTED 2002, 2003, 2004

ISBN 1 86054 182 8

Manufactured in Singapore

10 9 8 7 6 5 4

CONTENTS

SECTION TWO: HEALTH CARE
By Virginia Richardson

8. ANATOMY AND PHYSIOLOGY

The skeleton; The teeth; The digestive system (The mouth; The stomach; The small intestine; The large intestine; The caecum; The colon); The respiratory system; The cardiovascular system; The sense organs (The eye; The ear); The urinary system; The reproductive system (The male; The female); The skin and scent marking glands.

9. A-Z OF RABBIT DISEASES

Abscess; Aggression; Allergies; Alopecia; Amputation; Anorexia; Antibiotic-induced diarrhoea; Arthritis; Auto immune disease; Barbering; Bladder stones; Bloat; Blue fur; Caecal tympany; Caecotrophy; Candidiasis; Castration; Cataract; Cellulitis; Cheyletiella; Coccidiosis; Conjunctivitis; Coprophagy; Corneal ulceration; Cryptorchidism; Cystic mastitis; Cystitis; Demodectic mange; Dewlap; Diabetes; Diarrhoea; Dribbling; Dystocia; Ear mites; Endometrial hyperplasia; Endometrial venous aneurysm; Entropion; Eye; False pregnancy; Fleas; Floppy rabbit syndrome; Flystrike; Fractures; Gastric stasis; Haematuria; Haemorrhagic viral disease; Hairballs; Head tilt; Heart disease; Heat stroke; Incisor malocclusion; Intervertebral disc disease; Jawbone; Kidney failure; Lead poisoning; Liver; Malocclusion; Mammary gland neoplasia; Mastitis; Middle ear infection; Moulting; Mucoid enteritis; Myxomatosis; Nail disorders; Nasal discharge; Obesity; Osteomyelitis; Ovariohysterectomy; Paralysis; Paresis; Pasteurellosis; Pododermatitis; Potassium deficiency; Pseudopregnancy; Pyometra; Quadriplegia; Rabbit rings; Rabbit syphilis; Red urine; Retrobulbar abscess; Ringworm; Sludgy Bladder; Snuffles; Sore hocks; Spinal cord injury; Splay leg; Sticky bottom syndrome; Stroke; Tear duct infection; Testicular wounds; Ticks; Torticollis; Urine scalding; Urinary calculi; Uterine adenocarcinoma; Vent disease; Viral haemorrhagic disease; Warts; Womb cancer; Worms; Wry neck; X-rays; Yeast infection; Zoonoses.

SECTION THREE: RABBIT BREEDS
By Meg Brown

10. THE RABBIT COAT

The fur groups; Judging sections; Colour.

11. THE BREEDS

Types of rabbit; Introduction; Rabbit breeds (Alaska; American;

Angora; Argente Champagne; Astrex; Beaver; Beige; Belgian Hare;
Beveren; Black And Tan; Blanc de Bouscat; Blanc de Chauny;
Blanc de Hotot; Blanc à L'Oural; Blanc de Termonde; Blanc de
Vendee; Bourbonais Grey; Brown Chestnut Of Lorraine;
Californian; Chaudry; Chifox; Chinchilla; Cinnamon; Deilenaar;
Dutch; Tri-colour Dutch; English Butterfly; English Silver; Fauve de
Bourgogne; Old English Red; Fee de Marbourg; Flemish Giant;
Florida White; American Fox; Silver Foxes; Swiss Fox; Giant British
Rabbit; Golden Glavcot; Grey Pearl Of Hal; Ham Blue; Harlequin
or Japanese; Havana; Himalayan; The Large Himalayan or Russe;
Hooded Rabbit; Husumer; Land Kaninchen; Lilac or Dutch
Gouwenaar; Grey Swiss; Lops; Lorraine Rabbit; The Lynx;
Netherland Dwarf; New Zealand White; New Zealand Red; British
New Zealand Red; New Zealand Black; Opossum; Palamino; Giant
Papillon; Smoke Pearl; Perlfee; Picard or Giant Normand; Polish;
The Rexes; Rhinelander; Rhone Rabbit; Sable; Sable de Vosges;
Marten Sable or Zibeline; Sachsen Gold or Karlsbader Goldloh;
St Nicholas Blue; Sallander; Satin; Siberians; Silver Marten (USA);
The Sitka; The Squirrel; Swan Rabbit; Thrianta; Thuringer; Vienna;
Grey Vienna; Wachtebeke Rabbit; The Lion Rabbit.

12. EXHIBITING RABBITS

Judging difficulties; Rabbit identification; Do's and don'ts
of stewarding; Show etiquette; Ringing your rabbit;
Setting up a show; The judge; Pet rabbit shows;
Importing rabbits; Judging Lops.

APPENDICES

1. Glossary
2. Metrication table
3. Useful addresses

PREFACE

"A Book," said Alice "is nothing unless it has conversations and pictures."
Lewis Carroll.

I agree with Alice, and so, while the object of this book is to be helpful and informative, I have included some lighter asides to reflect the fun that is so much a part of owning a rabbit.

The rabbit is friendly, harmless, easy to feed and lives longer than some of the smaller popular pets; however, taking on any pet animal without thinking through the responsibilities involved is absolutely not fair. The rabbit has taken third place in many a Popular Pets Poll, yet, even now, pet rabbits are still being neglected or abandoned by their owners.

The estimated lifespan of a rabbit is three to four years, but they can, and do, live much longer, although exhibition rabbits tend to have a shorter life expectancy because they can become stressed out.

The rabbit does not annoy neighbours by barking or growling, nor does it give raucous calls at dawn like the cockerel. Its vocabulary is almost non-existent, although it can utter a high-pitched scream when afraid and a low growling noise when pleased. It can be a nuisance if allowed to roam in the garden, especially into the neighbours' gardens, and many a beautiful friendship has perished over a hole in the garden fence! Rabbits seem to flourish in the belief that the greens are always greener on the other side and I can remember the opening lines of a poem about this – *Rabbit in my cabbage patch*:

> O Bunny base,
> Why do this harm,
> With charming face,
> And whiskered charm?

Rabbits have affected people in other ways. The poet and author Robert Graves wrote this *Epitaph on an Unfortunate Artist*.

> He found a formula for drawing comic rabbits
> This formula for drawing comic rabbits paid.
> So in the end he couldn't change the tragic habits
> This formula for drawing comic rabbits made!

CHAPTER I

THE HISTORY OF THE RABBIT

The history of the rabbit, and its domestication, is absolutely fascinating. Experts say that the rabbit goes back about 4,000 years and originated in Spain. Fossilised remains have been found, mostly in Spain and Portugal. In Turkey, there still exists a sphinx that was erected around 1500 BC which stands on two rabbit figures. It is generally agreed that the rabbit arrived in the UK with the Normans in 1066, but it has also been suggested that it came over with the Romans.

Although it appears in art and literature in the Middle Ages as a so-called 'domestic' animal, the rabbit was kept in captivity long before this. When the Phoenicians, trading by sea, reached Spain in 1100 BC, they noticed this small animal and called it Shofon, which also means Hyrax, and this was translated, by various Biblical scholars, as coney. The word cony, or coney, meaning rabbit, has been in use since the Middle Ages and came from Old French, Anglo-French and Latin; it is still used in statutes and in heraldry. It originally referred to the adult rabbit, while the word rabbit was used only for the young rabbit and came from a dialect of either Old French or Low Dutch, or both.

It should be noted, however, that a Hyrax is not a coney. The Hyrax, which is not unlike the coney, has a seven-month gestation period which produces only one youngster. It lives in holes in rocks and has rubber-like pads on its feet for ease in rock climbing.

1. THE GREAT ESCAPE

In the first century AD the Romans kept rabbits, or conies, in walled gardens together with hares and dormice. The dormice were kept in cages hung on the walls and were considered to be a great delicacy to eat. This method of keeping rabbits and hares together was complicated, as rabbits and hares are not friendly, and hares live on the ground surface while rabbits are burrowers. Escapes into the surrounding country were inevitable. Rabbits multiplied and spread, with the help of the Roman Legions marching through Europe making their Empire. The soldiers fed on the rabbits and used their pelts for warm clothing. Pliny, the great naturalist, gives much valuable information about the rabbit at that time. He wrote that a single pair let loose in the Balearic Islands multiplied so greatly that the islanders appealed to the Emperor Hadrian (AD 76-135) to send help to resettle the islanders elsewhere. The ferret was used then, as it is today, for catching rabbits, and ferrets have now also become a popular pet.

2. RABBIT GARDENS

A system of rabbit gardens was introduced to Britain by the Normans. The Norman invaders, as part of their entourage, had a warrener and his ferrets – and the surnames Warren and Warrener are good reminders of this period in history. The rabbit warren was a small, enclosed field surrounded by a deep ditch, and a high turf back on which were planted gorse and blackberry bushes. These were also known as coney garths or coneyries. The ditches were eventually discontinued, as they were a considerable hazard to the King's horsemen and their horses during Royal hunts.

Escape from warrens was easy, and soon the rabbit became free game for yeomen and serfs. However, the penalties for being caught indulging in this activity were extremely severe, and remained so for centuries – it is on record that a poacher in 1814 caught netting a hare and rabbit was transported for seven years.

> *DID YOU KNOW?*
> *There is in existence a remarkable French manuscript of AD 1393 depicting ladies hunting conies with bows and arrows and lap dogs. A gentle pursuit indeed!*

3. ISLAND RABBITS

Between the 13th and 14th centuries, early explorers and trading ships, especially those belonging to the Dutch East Indies Company, populated islands on the main sea-roads with rabbits, which could be a valuable source of food for distressed and shipwrecked sailors. In 1652 the explorer Van Riebeck put eight rabbits on Robin Island, off Capetown (originally known as Seal Island), which had abounded with penguins and birds, and later sheep and cattle were introduced. However, the eight rabbits multiplied at such a rate that all vegetation was destroyed. The cattle and sheep had to be removed and in 1658 convicts were sent instead!

The practice of putting rabbits on islands to provide a food supply was common in Europe – the Portuguese, for example, also colonised small islands with goats as well as rabbits, for the same reasons. Henry IV had enclosures at Clichy, now a Paris suburb; Elizabeth I had her rabbit island on the Thames; and, near Berlin, the island of Pfauninsal, once known as Kaninchesswarder or Rabbit Island, was used for rabbit keeping by the 18th-century king of Prussia, Frederick the Great. There is a large island off the North Coast of Scotland that is also known as Rabbit Island but, unfortunately, there is no clear evidence of it being used for breeding rabbits – no-one seems to know why it has the name, not even the locals!

4. DOMESTICATION

Under those island conditions, rabbits kept their wild characteristics; domestication was brought about by monks. Because they lived in seclusion, the monks appreciated an easily obtainable meat supply, and their need to find a food suitable for Lent caused them to fall back on an item much loved by the Romans – the unborn young or newly born of the rabbit does, called Laurices. This strange taste, combined with the need to keep the rabbits within the monastery walls, created the conditions that led to proper domestication. Rabbits kept in garden warrens or coneyries would have retained their timidity and wild instincts, while those kept in monasteries would, in time, have become fairly tame.

It was uneconomical for the monks to kill the pregnant doe to obtain the youngsters, so the newly-born litters saved the life of the doe and made it possible for her to produce a succession of progeny. The first experiments took place in French monasteries. Under such conditions, selection of breeding stock became inevitable.

> *DID YOU KNOW?*
> *The earliest picture of a White Rabbit, dated 1530, hangs in the Louvre – Madonna with a Rabbit, by Titian.*

5. SELECTIVE BREEDING

It was not until the middle of the 16th century that black, white and piebald rabbits appear in literature. Agricola, a monk from Verona, Italy, who was responsible for his monastery's gardens and livestock, wrote about them. He also mentioned rabbits that were bred in Verona which were four times the normal size; these were probably the forerunner of the Giant Rabbits, the Flemish Giant and the Patagonia – a very large, ugly rabbit.

In fact, Patagonia rabbits did not come from Patagonia but were so named to give them rarity value. The popular belief was that Patagonia was a land of giants and ogres. They are also known as the Angevin, the Belier and the Ram.

Of the two kinds of rabbit – those bred in a warren, and the domesticated type kept in the monasteries – it was the domesticated type that spread to other countries first. For example, the earliest document relating to a wild rabbit is a woodcut in Germany dated 1423, but the importation of domestic rabbits occurred 300 years earlier. In 1194 the Abbot Carvey asked the Abbot of Solignac in France to send him two pairs of rabbits to Germany. Had he been sensible, he would have asked for one buck and two does!

6. FUR COATS

By the 17th century, domestic rabbit breeding was in full swing in England. In 1631, a silver-grey rabbit was reported, which was described as silver-grey with a mixture of black and white hairs. It was highly valued, as rabbit fur was in demand for ornamentation, and for the linings of cloaks, hoods, and bed covers. In the same year, 1631, the fur rabbit was described by Gervase Markham:

"Ye shall not as in other cattle, look to their shape but to their richness and select only the largest and goodliest conies ye can get, and for the richness of the skins that is the richness which hath the equal mixture and blacke and white hairs together, yet the blacke overshadowing the white. The fur should be thick deep and shining. They are of the body much fatter and larger and when other skins are worth 2-3 pence, they are worth 2 shillings."

In the late 15th century, under Henry VIII, there were laws governing dress and, with the wearing of rabbit fur, a distinction was made between ladies and 'loose' women, the latter being forbidden to wear rabbit fur in their hoods. An alternative was to use vair, which was a fur obtained from a variety of squirrel with a grey back and white belly. This had been much used in the 13th and 14th centuries as a trimming or lining for garments – weasel and stoat/ermine fur was also used.

When this legislation was renewed by Henry's daughter, Elizabeth I, no-one whose income was less than £100 per year could wear the fur of 'conies'. She did, however, have a dwarf attendant of whom she was very fond. She called her "my Tartarean Woman" and gave her three cassocks of black velvet trimmed with silver coney furs.

In 1580, an itinerant Puritan preacher, named John Darrel, took to a new career of casting out of devils, demons and evil spirits. He had an apprentice, named Somers, whom he taught to simulate fits before an audience. Darrel then got to work casting out his evil spirits. However, Darrel's apprentice grew tired of this and wanted to be set free, so Darrel let him go and found him a place "to keep Silver Haired Conies". Was this rabbit the ancestor of all our silver-haired rabbits and was Somers possibly one of the first commercial breeders?

In 1621, Anton Van Leeuwen Hoek (one of the improvers of the microscope) wrote to the Royal Society mentioning that his compatriots were crossing white does with wild bucks because the market required coloured furs. Breeders fought and quarrelled over the silver-haired rabbit's ancestry and colours.

7. RABBIT CHARMS

Rabbits were bred in their thousands and, by 1870, skins exported to Europe were worth £5 per dozen. By 1880, all parts of the rabbit were in use, with waste fur being used for manure, and paws being sold to Scandinavia for charms. The American African slaves had the same idea – "Lil rabbit foot do yer charm, and keep me all this day from harm; as I have no time to pray, watch over me all this day."

Gardeners still use tails fixed to canes for cross-pollination of plants, and glue from rabbit skins is still used to fix book bindings, tapestry and embroidery pictures and to mend violins. Rabbit feet have also been used to apply cosmetics. Even today Scandinavia is a huge importer of rabbit paws from the USA.

In various parts of the world some people still use the exclamation "Rabbits, rabbits!" on the first day of every month before they speak to another human being. It is, in fact, a corruption of the word orabitis, which means 'Ye shall pray'. This word was used in pre-Reformation church services in the UK and has survived as "rabbits" in country districts. This custom is supposed to bring good luck.

It is astonishing to learn that the spread of the rabbit was total, throughout England and Wales, between 1880-1890. In Scotland, it was not quite complete until the

Prize lop-eared rabbits – winners for weight and length of ears.

beginning of this century. Neither rabbits nor hares were seen in Argyll until General Wade built military roads at the time of the Jacobite Rebellions in 1745.

In 1792, Bewick wrote that "Rabbits are now divided into four categories". These were large, and small, tame, Piebald, Angora, and a remarkable variety known as the Muscovy or hooded rabbit. Later, Lop-eared types were added to the list. The rabbit has now spread worldwide, introduced from Europe to Northern Africa, Australia, New Zealand, Chile, islands in the Pacific and Atlantic, and America and Canada, and there are now 25 different varieties of Rabbit or Oryctolagus Cuniculi (a burrower).

8. THE EMPEROR'S PATRONAGE

Probably the most famous rabbit breeder of all time was Napoleon III, nephew of Napoleon I. During his imprisonment in the Castle of Ham in 1840, following his failure to raise popular support, the future Emperor became a keen gardener and rabbit breeder. When he became Emperor in 1852, he planned to build small workers' houses, complete with garden and backyard. But it was not until after the American War in 1856 that his plan for smallholdings materialised; each smallholder who received a house was obliged to breed rabbits. The result of this rabbit farming was the production of millions of pelts which were used by the army for cloak linings.

In South West France, rabbit farming became more and more important, and it was in the working-class areas of this region that Napoleon III created colonies of smallholdings. In due course, these smallholders became the owners of their land. Initially, each had 2,500 square metres, to allow the holder enough ground to produce fodder for his rabbits, pigs and goats. However, it became impossible to give so much ground to each smallholder, so the area was reduced to 600-700 sq

Rabbit breeds exhibited at the Crystal Palace show in 1872.

metres. The smallholder had to give up his pigs and goats – but Napoleon compelled them to continue rabbit breeding.

In 1866, 1,000 of those smallholdings were constructed for the sum of 1,000,000 francs in gold – Napoleon personally donated 300,000 francs. Consequently, France has become one of the largest producers of rabbit meat and fur. All wastage from the pelts goes into the manufacture of felt. It takes 40 rabbit skins to make one fur felt hat.

DID YOU KNOW?
Felt for hats, in the famous hat-making industry in Lincoln, for example, is made of
unwoven wool and angora rabbit hair and fur. It is matted together by heat and
moisture, the fibres becoming so closely entwined that a compact cloth surface is
produced – felt. Roofing felt is made from the same process, although the material is
produced by also mixing in coal-tar or asphalt.

---

9. 19th-CENTURY RABBIT CLASSIFICATION

In the 19th century, before the rabbit became an exhibition type – and
apart from the other classifications of small, tame sorts, lop-eared sorts,
piebalds and angoras – rural communities classified them as:

- Sweethearts
- Warreners
- Parkers
- Hedgehogs.

The Sweethearts were sleek, well fed, well housed, tamed and living a life of ease
with nothing to do but eat and grow fat and help to fatten their human devourers.
The Warreners inhabited the sandy warren where their burrows honeycombed the
earth and afforded a rich spoil for poachers and other predators. The Parkers were
to be found on gentlemen's estates where they were more protected within the
boundaries of the park. The Hedgehogs (not the spiny ones) lived in holes in banks
and all sorts of out-of-the-way places like chalk pits. They wandered about in a very
unsettled manner and were the 'gypsies' of their kind.

CHAPTER 2

YOUR FIRST
RABBIT

"It is a poor man that has not hobby."

The rabbit is known as the poor man's cattle, for it can provide food and clothing and is, above all, economical to keep. However, it is important to remember that the rabbit is completely dependent on you for its wellbeing and that all its needs will have to be catered for and understood. You will need to study the rabbit's habits so that you can recognise any signs of distress or illness, and you will need to find time for feeding, cleaning, and grooming. Many a rabbit has been abandoned because the owner has not been aware of what pet care means. But, if you are committed to becoming a responsible owner, it can be a most rewarding hobby indeed.

1. CHOOSING A RABBIT

Rabbits can be acquired from pet shops, rabbit breeders or show exhibitors. It is worth noting that, very often, stock which does not come up to show standard ends up in the pet shop. You can, of course, contact your nearest rabbit club or their main body, the Rabbit Council. All rabbit governing bodies will be only too delighted to help. They can provide names and addresses of the nearest rabbit club in your area and also the nearest rabbit breeder. Much information is available on the internet.

Agricultural shows are good places in which to find a rabbit section. Do not be afraid to ask any of the breeders to give you a guided tour, for this is the best way to

14

find a rabbit you really admire. Rabbit people are only too happy to talk about their hobby; they are very friendly people and will go out of their way to help.

Be honest with the breeder and tell him whether you want pet, breeding or show stock. Show animals have very exacting standards – and are also more expensive.

DOE OR BUCK?

Stock is best purchased at about 12 to 16 weeks old. At this age, the rabbit will be past the stage of falling prey to the stress-related ailments which can affect the younger animals, and yet it is still not an adult. Young rabbits settle into a new environment better than adults.

Bucks are more easily trained. Neutered bucks and neutered does can live quite happily together. Does can live together in small groups provided they have space and, better still, if they come from the same litter. Some people advise keeping rabbits in the colony system, but I do not think this is wise.

NEUTERING STOCK

It is not so long ago that the neutering of rabbits was first introduced. The reasons given for neutering by V. Richardson, MA, VET. MB, MRCVS in the paper *Rabbit Health Care, Issue I, Vol I* make interesting reading. By the age of five years, up to 50 per cent of female rabbits who have not been neutered develop uterine carcinoma. Neutering also removes all behavioural problems such as mounting, aggression and spraying and, of course, it prevents unwanted litters. Neutered rabbits are also easier to train, particularly in the use of litter trays and, with bucks, there is less smell. Bucks can be castrated at about three to four months when the testicles descend. This is either done through a simple operation or, as is the practice in America, by using a chemical injection into the testicles. Does are neutered at six months. The smaller breeds such as Dwarf rabbits can be neutered at four months.

WHAT BREED?

If you are planning to buy a rabbit as a child's pet, the most suitable breeds are the Himalayan, which is a small, easily handled and wonderfully placid rabbit with no vices, and the well-known Dutch rabbit (probably the most popular), which is also good-tempered and easily-handled. The new breed called the Lion rabbit is ideal, being small and placid and not too costly.

My first rabbit, as a child, was a blue Dutch. Unfortunately, it was mated by a wild buck and produced a fine litter of five. The doe was a good mother but I do remember the litter being quite untameable, they were so wild. Dad said: "You can't keep wild creatures in a hutch, it isn't kind to keep them cooped up." So to the wood they went, where they soon settled and multiplied.

WHAT TO LOOK FOR

If you buy from a pet shop, you must ask to handle the rabbit in order to examine it. The rabbit you buy should be around 12 weeks old. Remember that, if you are buying a pet for a child, it must be of a breed which is suitable in size and temperament and be easy to handle. Check for the following signs of good health:

- Coat condition – is it clean and glossy with health? Make sure there are no signs of mites, and look to see if the coat is clean around the anus, with no evidence of diarrhoea.

15

- Eyes – they should be bright, with no discharge.
- Nose – damp, but no discharge.
- Front paws – look at the inside of front paws. Are they wet or matted? If so, the rabbit probably has a runny nose, and is wiping its nose with its paws.
- Teeth – check to see if they protrude, or are crooked. A rabbit's teeth should meet evenly. Young rabbits' teeth are pointed until they begin to gnaw; after this they become even and should meet together evenly.

Any pet in first-class condition will help you to succeed in the hobby of rabbit keeping or showing.

> *RABBITS AND THE LAW*
> *Legally, rabbits aged under eight weeks should not be sold. To buy a rabbit you must be at least 18 years old both in Europe and in the USA.*

2. RABBITS AND CHILDREN

Someone once wrote: "A rabbit is an ideal model for teaching children benevolence." Whether or not this is true I do not know, but the supervision of children who look after pets is essential. It would also be extremely foolish to buy a pet rabbit for any child who is not old enough to understand its needs. Also, youngsters may tire of looking after a live pet. An Australian rabbit breeder tells a story that is repeated all too often.

"I bought my sons a rabbit after they promised they would take care of it. As usual, I ended up with the responsibility. Thoroughly exasperated, I asked: 'How many times do you think that rabbit would have died if I hadn't looked after it?' My 12-year-old replied, 'Once'."

Having said that, I have observed that children do have the ability to build up a loving relationship with animals and they seem to understand each another in a way that no adult can experience. Adults are always looking for problems even when none exist.

3. RESPONSIBILITIES

If you seriously consider the demands of keeping rabbits – for example, in terms of time and cost (including your holiday arrangements) – and you are keen to follow professional advice (reading this book is a good start!), then there is every chance that you can become a successful rabbit owner.

Not everyone thinks the responsibilities through, however, and every year rabbits are found abandoned. Recently, I was alerted to an abandoned rabbit; it was found in a nearby field complete with food dish and a bag of rabbit food! Fortunately this rabbit, a chinchilla, was found a good home. However, that kind of irresponsibility simply adds to the problems that the animal welfare organisations must deal with.

Remember, a rabbit lives, on average, for three to five years – sometimes longer – and it is your responsibility to care for it throughout its life. A pet rabbit, well looked after by a loving owner, can live to a good old age – up to 10 years or more. I have an old doe, now aged 13 years, and her advanced age has turned her into a holy terror!

> **DID YOU KNOW?**
> *One record-breaking rabbit was Floppy who was born in 1964 and died on June 29th 1983, aged 18 years 10 months. The long life of this Tasmanian rabbit has now been surpassed by a New Zealand White rabbit aged 24 years, bred by a Mr Fiske in Nova Scotia.*

4. BASIC REQUIREMENTS

A rabbit is a relatively low-maintenance animal, and its needs are modest. You will need:

- A hutch or cage (see Chapter Three).
- A food dish – earthenware bowls, such as cats and dogs use, are ideal. Plastic dishes are too light, and tend to get kicked around.
- A gravity-fed water bottle. As rabbits drink a lot of water, it would be wise to buy a good-sized one.
- A regular supply of rabbit food and hay from a reputable supplier (see Chapter Four).
- Rabbits do not require toys, like other small pets rodents such as hamsters, rats or mice, but they do need something to gnaw on. Rabbit teeth keep on growing, and rabbits need something to chew on to keep their teeth in order.

Mme Jouffrey D'Abban, a very famous French rabbit breeder, wrote that "a rabbit without a branch to gnaw is like a dog without a bone." A piece of wood will do, provided it has not been creosoted or painted. If you do not supply a branch or small log, your rabbit will start on its hutch – and then your shed.

5. HANDLING

The correct way to pick up a rabbit is with one hand under its rump and the other hand across the back of its head, clasping it closely to your chest for security. Never, ever lift it by the ears! It can however be grasped firmly by one hand on the loose skin behind the shoulders. It is essential that children are taught correct handling procedures.

It is also possible to 'hypnotise' a rabbit: if you lie it on its back, gently stroking its chest, abdomen and the sides of its head, it will go into a trance-like state. This is not of any practical use, except perhaps during minor surgery, or for simply showing off what you can do!

6. RABBITS AND OTHER PETS

Rabbits are very territorial and do not like sharing their allotted space with any other animal. They have, however, been known to live quite amicably with guinea pigs. From my own experience in the past with an English Lop living in the house, I soon discovered that it would not tolerate either my dog, a Whippet, or my cat. The hearthrug was the main bone of contention – and the cat and dog soon learned not to place a paw on it. Hefty kicks from the rabbit's back feet quickly taught them that it was not their place. I cannot envisage a rabbit living in harmony with a hamster, a gerbil, a rat or even a mouse, although I have known of a rat who shared a hutch with a rabbit without any fuss.

CHAPTER 3

HOUSING
YOUR RABBIT

Shelter is one of the two most important things in life – the other is food; no-one would disagree with that. Therefore, before you buy your rabbit or rabbits you must have somewhere to house them.

1. THE RABBIT HUTCH
The simplest way is the traditional rabbit hutch (the word comes from the French 'huche', a chest on four legs). With the advance in packaging, gone are the days of the old tea chests and barrels on trestles. Basically the hutch is a large wooden box standing on its side supported by four sturdy legs. It is divided into two compartments: the smaller one for shelter and sleeping and also for somewhere private if you have a breeding doe.

The hutch should have a gap in the partition to allow the rabbit easy access from one compartment to the other. It should be at least 18 ins (45.7 cms) off the ground; this will deter the advances of wild rabbits and, of course, their fleas, which can jump at least 7 ins (17.7 cms). The roof should have a slight overhang to keep out the weather. The front of the hutch should have two doors; one should be solid for the sleeping place and the other should have a good, strong, small-gauge wire (twill weld is excellent). The outside of the hutch should be weatherproofed – and do not forget the underside.

Ready-made hutches are readily available but care is needed when choosing for, although some are reasonably priced, not all are well made. This is where a good DIY person scores over the rest of us. Beech-wood is best as it is non-absorbent, therefore ideal for hutch building. Above all, the hutch should be well built of seasoned wood. All joints and fittings must fit perfectly with no draughts. Place your hutches facing south in a sheltered position.

The size of the hutch depends, naturally, on the breed and size of rabbit; giant rabbits, like Flemish and Lotharingers etc., need more space. The normal size is 3 ft (91.5 cms) x 3 ft (91.5 cms) x 2 ft (61 cms) and 6 ft (1.83 metres) x 4 ft (1.22 metres) x 3 ft (91.5 cms) for larger breeds. The height should be high enough for large rabbits with upstanding ears – the Flemish Giant, for example, has ears that are 7-8 inches long (17.7 cms to 20 cms), and the Belgian Hare, with its very upright carriage, would also need a larger hutch.

Legislation is now underway to stipulate hutch sizes. These are likely to be as follows:

- Does and litter up to 5 weeks: 0.56 square metres (6 sq ft).
- Does and litter up to 7 weeks: 0.74 square metres (8 sq ft).
- Weaned adults: 0.56 square metres (6 sq ft).

If you intend to keep more than one rabbit, a small garden shed could be a help. A wooden shed with a floor and window is not all that expensive, and it provides additional shelter for the rabbits and owner. It need not be very large but it is important that it has good ventilation. A shed 8 ft (2.43 metres) x 10 ft (3 metres) can hold three to four hutches quite comfortably along one of the long walls. It is important to have the hutches clear of the floor with enough room to sweep the floor.

Again, it should be weatherproofed and, where possible, sited on a cement or brick foundation. All hutches and sheds should be made impregnable as far as rodents (mice, rats, squirrels etc.) are concerned, as they can create havoc in a rabbitry. Keep all food in storage bins with good, well-fitting lids.

2. ALTERNATIVE HOUSING

Commercial breeders use hutches with wire mesh floors of small-gauge wire and a metal tray underneath to catch droppings. These are easily cleaned (a blowlamp is very useful to burn off bits of fur etc.).

In suitable circumstances, rabbits may be kept loose in areas enclosed with wire netting which should be at least 4 ft (1.2 metres) high and sunk in the ground for at least 2-3 ft (60 cms to 90 cms). Several small hutches could be kept within. Also a few drainpipes of at least 4 ins diameter for shelter and play can be added. It should be noted that rabbits in this type of enclosure tend to revert to the wild, becoming more timid and less tame.

Housing depends greatly on climatic conditions. I live on the west coast of Scotland where the biggest enemy is dampness. It seems to penetrate everywhere and living on any seaboard will bring this problem. Dampness is one of the big drawbacks in rabbit breeding, and this also applies to bad husbandry, i.e. wet or sodden bedding.

During the war, I was stationed outside Naples in Italy. There I saw an orchard in which rabbits were kept in a deep hole, about 6-8 ft (1.8 to 2.4 metres) deep, lined with netting. The rabbits seemed quite lively. The owner came along and tossed in three whole cabbages but I did not see any other sort of feeding!

In Africa, I saw rabbits housed in wire cages suspended about 4 ft above the ground and shaded with a coarse thatched roof which had poles at each corner and a crossbar for cage support, something like a carport.

3. LOCATING THE HUTCH

Whatever housing arrangement you decide upon, it is important to make sure that the hutches are well made and well sited. The same goes for the rabbit shed or carport.

Shade is extremely important in the summer and in warmer climates. As rabbits have fur coats and no sweat glands they are more sensitive to heat than cold and can only lose heat through their respiration. So, ideally, a rabbitry shed would have an overhang for added shade.

Trees will keep the sun out and increase the moisture level which cools the air around the hutch and there is, actually, a certain tree that can be grown which is excellent to have alongside your rabbitry. It is called *Catalpa Bignoides* or 'Big Bean Tree' and it grows 8-10 ft (2.4 to 3 metres) high, with large leaves and white blossom. It is fairly common in the USA and in some gardens in England, and for rabbit keepers its main virtue is that it is strongly repellent against all kinds of gnats and flies.

Another repellent is the *physaloides* or 'shoo fly' plant. Mixed mint leaves hung up in bunches in the rabbitry are also good fly repellents.

The rabbit hutch should be sturdy, spacious and weather-proofed.

Travelling box

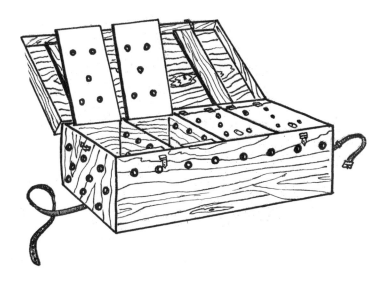

Elderberry trees and bog myrtle bushes are other well-known fly repellents. Also, do not despise the spider and his web in your rabbitry, as it is the cleanest and quickest way to get rid of flies. Of course there are fly-sprays, but these are rarely suitable where livestock is kept, and fly papers are effective but a nuisance as they invariably stick to the breeder's hair! A small amount of paraffin put into containers and out of the rabbit's reach is an excellent repellent; flies are attracted to the paraffin, fall in and are drowned. Cloves hung in clusters in the shed are also very effective, and a sponge soaked in citronella and hung above the door or windows repels flies, ants and gnats etc.

4. THE RABBIT CAGE
House rabbits are becoming increasingly popular as pets, and although they have a reasonable amount of freedom, they still need somewhere to sleep, and somewhere to go when you are out of the house. A large wire cage, at least 6 ft long by 3 ft wide and 3 ft high, with a resting board covering the wire floor, and with some bedding, such as newspaper or shredded paper, on a floorboard is ideal. There should also be a water-bottle attached to the cage and room for a litter tray. There are some really up-market indoor hutches newly available. They are designed to look like a piece of furniture, and they are pretty expensive, but the talented handyman may be able to copy the idea.

5. THE MORANT HUTCH

The breeder with one or two rabbits and possessing a small paddock, or even a fair-sized lawn, will find a grazing hutch very useful during spring and summer. The most popular type is known as a Morant hutch, designed by Major J.F. Morant of Essex in the 1880s. It resembles the triangular poultry ark. The sides and floor are of strong, one-inch netting fastened to a strong wooden frame. One end is boarded in to afford shelter, with a sleeping shelf which is raised above the ground. The door to the hutch is at the end of the boarded section. A bolt hole to the run can be closed to keep the rabbit in the enclosed part. The usual size is about 6 ft long. It must be easy to move around, since the whole idea is to move it about on grass of a suitable growth, about one to three inches. The hutch must be moved every day.

It is now rarely used by exhibitors, as strong sunlight fades coats. However, it does make a good summer residence for a rabbit. But beware if there is more than one occupant – fighting could break out.

6. BEDDING

I find that a thick layer of newspaper on the floor, with sawdust or shavings on the top and then straw or chaff on top of that, is ideal. When it comes to cleaning out, remove the whole lot wrapped in the paper and dispose of it. This saves much time. An excellent source of bedding is available in autumn – collect clean dry leaves and store them in open weave sacks. Lawn clippings can also be used as long as they are well dried and kept in a dry place. The leaves and the clippings can also be used for fodder.

Cardboard boxes make wonderful nest-boxes and young and old rabbits like to sleep in them. They are large with a round opening in one end which provides ingress and exits. They are perfect in size for medium-sized rabbits of 4-5 lbs. Invariably, the boxes get chewed to bits but the supply of such boxes is endless. Any supermarket or cafe will keep empties on request.

> *DID YOU KNOW?*
> *Newspapers are extremely useful as bedding in hutches, for they deter mites. They do not like the printer's ink!*

7. CLEANING THE HUTCH

For wooden hutches, beech-wood is ideal as it is a non-absorbent wood. Every breeder has his own ideas on cleaning out. To render the inside of the hutch waterproof, it can be painted over with coats of the varnish used by yacht builders – but obviously, it must be non-poisonous in case the rabbit licks or chews it.

Floors are the biggest problem. What is the best system of keeping them dry and clean? There is no doubt about the answer – a daily clean-out. Cleanliness and a dry hutch are essential. I have wooden floors on my hutches. They get swept out with a rough, tough, hand-brush. I then sprinkle a powdered dustbin cleanser lightly on the bare floor. I cover this with a thick wad of newspaper with a topping of woodshavings or shredded paper. When I change the floor covering, I just roll it up in an instant and burn it. Small garden incinerators are ideal, especially the type which looks like a dustbin with a well-fitting lid and a small central chimney. It usually has four sturdy legs and two rows of holes around the bottom. It is not very expensive and is a boon to the rabbit keeper.

Any wet patches on the hutch floor or corners can be safely sprayed using a packet of borax to a bucket of water. This removes any odour and helps to dry out the wet area. It also helps as a fly deterrent.

In the toilet corner of the hutch a small litter tray is very helpful in keeping the hutch clean. Gardeners' seedling trays are ideal, being easy to handle and to clean. Put a layer of newspaper in the bottom and cover with a thick layer of sawdust.

Wire cages usually have a wire floor with a metal tray underneath, which makes cleaning fairly easy. With a wire floor it is a good idea to have a wood piece to put in the rabbit's favourite corner because it is more comfortable for the rabbit to sleep on than wire. All wire doors and floors collect a great deal of dust and fluff and a small blowlamp is essential to remove this – but do remember to take your rabbit out of the hutch first. You do not want it barbecued!

8. DISPOSING OF HUTCH-CLEANINGS

There are a number of misconceptions in relation to disposing of hutch-cleanings, and this is an area that needs to be clarified.

Do the woodshavings in hutch-cleanings harm soil?

The answer, in a word, is NO, especially when used correctly. Woodshavings and sawdust are much maligned by gardeners, which is a great shame. In particular, woodshavings do not:

- Introduce harmful organisms into soil.
- Encourage wireworms and other spoil pests.
- Make the soil more acid.

Do the woodshavings remove nitrogen from the soil?

Fresh, raw sawdust or woodshavings dug into soil does produce an immediate but temporary loss of nitrogen. This is because the carbon contained in the sawdust encourages bacterial growth which extracts nitrogen from the soil. As time passes, however, wood wastes go on to replace the nitrogen and other nutrients, and greatly improve soil texture. To avoid the problem of the initial nitrogen loss, there are several options:

- Use hutch-cleanings as a mulch for established crops. Hutch-cleanings used in this way conserve soil moisture, control weeds, improve soil temperature, eventually improve soil structure and help to keep plants clean and free from disease.
- Add some nitrogen fertiliser at the same time as hutch-cleanings, e.g. sulphate of ammonia at about 4 per cent of the weight of the cleanings.
- Use hutch-cleanings for pea and bean crops. These are fairly independent of soil supplies of nitrogen.

WHY IS COMPOSTING HELPFUL?

Composting hutch-cleanings produces an excellent material for soil improvement. When added to the soil it encourages the growth of beneficial bacteria, fungi and worms, and helps make the plant foods in the soil available. Compost also improves soil texture and helps to retain soil moisture.

WHAT IS THE BEST WAY TO COMPOST HUTCH-CLEANINGS?

Because they decompose slowly, sawdust and woodshavings should be composted by themselves rather than on a general compost heap, unless hutch-cleanings constitute only 7-8 per cent of the total.

The compost heap itself should be built into a well-aerated heap when enough material is available. Water should be added if it becomes too dry, and it is also a good idea to add either a nitrogen fertiliser or a compost activator.

Hutch-cleanings do take a long time (9-12 months) to turn into good compost, but at the end of this time it will be highly prized by gardeners or allotment-holders.

Long ago, when I was new to rabbit keeping, I turfed the hutch floor. It was most satisfactory. I just replaced one turf with another. The farmer's field benefited as well. I had to give this up, however, when my rabbit population increased and turfing became very time-consuming (I combined rabbit keeping with a busy nursing career). In the end, I found that using newspaper, sawdust and straw was the easiest option.

CHAPTER 4

FEEDING RABBITS

1. Nutritional needs
2. How much to feed
3. Types of food

"God said unto Noah 'to everything that is upon the earth, wherein there is life, I have given every green herb for meat and it was so'."

Feeding is probably the most important aspect of rabbit keeping. It governs the wellbeing and condition of the rabbit, whether it is a pet or an exhibition animal. Most beginners, particularly children, tend to overfeed their pets and then they wonder why their rabbit is sick. Feeding once daily is quite enough; only pregnant rabbits and growing youngsters need extra food. Do feed at a regular time each day – the rabbit will soon catch on and conform to your timetable. A constant supply of water is essential, and this should be replaced daily. A good tip to keep the water from freezing in winter is to add a little salt, or a few drops of glycerine.

There is a golden rule about feeding. When you are buying a rabbit, be it from a pet shop or breeder, do ask what food has been given. Sudden changes in diet tend to be fatal, especially in young rabbits. Any change of diet must be done slowly, adding the new feed, a little at a time, on top of the usual feed. Also, be extremely careful if making up your own mix. You may think you know best, but many a breeder, even experienced breeders, have lost their entire stock because they thought their ideas were better than those of the experts.

1. NUTRITIONAL NEEDS

In the wild, rabbits have an endless supply of grasses and plants. They crop almost anything that grows but instinctively avoid poisonous plants. Wild rabbits invariably look in the pink of condition because wild herbage provides varying herbal qualities, for example some are astringent and some act as a laxative. Nature's mixtures cannot be bettered – but the modern rabbit keeper no longer roams fields and hedgerows with sack and scythe.

With the increase in commercial rabbit breeding and the easier way of feeding, most breeders of exhibition rabbits soon adopted pellets as a foodstuff. Pellets are a scientifically compounded feed, which includes vitamins, minerals, 17 per cent proteins, and 14 per cent ash, oils, grass meal, cereals, sunflower, linseed extract, etc. They produce rapid weight gain and growth in youngsters, which can then be marketed at 8-12 weeks old.

Rabbit foods sold as mixes are widely available. Some are good, some are very good and some pretty awful. If you are buying a loose mix in a pet shop, ask to see it before you buy. Take a handful and give it a good look. If it is made up of dusty, broken pellets, wheat chaff, broken cereal flakes, biscuit etc., forget it! There are many well-known brands available nowadays. The superior mixes contain dried vegetables such as carrots, peas, cabbage, and molasses. Molasses (black treacle) is a very good tonic. A small teaspoonful in the rabbit's drinking water is excellent, but do not overdo it, otherwise the rabbit will scour – in other words, have diarrhoea. All pelleted food and mixes should be kept in closed containers. Mice love mixes. There is no need to encourage them!

2. HOW MUCH TO FEED

A dwarf breed needs 2 oz per day of pellets or mixes and a large breed needs 4 oz per day. Find a cup or any container which holds the requisite amount, for it will save you having to weigh it every day. A few sunflower seeds scattered among the pellets are much appreciated by the rabbit and give a glorious shine to the coat.

3. TYPES OF FOOD

HAY

It is important to have a good bunch of fresh, clean hay available. It must be six months old before feeding – newly-cut hay must never be given. The hay can be tied in a bundle and fastened to the hutch well above the floor, or a simple manger can be made from an oblong piece of chicken wire, which can be fastened to the inside of the hutch door.

There is one caution to be noted regarding the hay. If it comes in long stalks it must be chopped into smaller lengths, because a long piece of hay can become tangled around the rabbit's paws. This can quickly form a hay rope which may tighten up and cut off blood supply to the foot. This can be very serious indeed, so inspect your rabbit daily.

If you are keeping pet rabbits, you will probably buy your hay from a pet shop, where it is probably sold in mini-bales. These are convenient, and are usually sterilised as well. Make sure the hay you feed is free from dust, is sweet-smelling, and has no trace of mouldiness. Barn allergy is an ailment caused by the rabbit inhaling mites, both alive and dead. Stored hay can contain 46,000 mites in a 27-kg bale. Note that meadow hay contains 60 per cent crude protein and dried nettles 96 per cent protein if cut before flowering.

BREAD
All scraps of bread should be dried off rock hard; it is no matter if it gets burnt as it is highly nutritious, very much appreciated by the rabbits and good for their teeth.

GREEN FEEDING
The wild rabbit in its natural state lives mainly on fresh and dried greenstuff and roots. The tame one is larger and grows faster. As it does not get the same exercise, it is not economic to feed it with the same food as the wild one.

DON'TS
Do not feed lettuce, cabbage, parsnips, frozen or wet greens, evergreens and bulbous plants. Lettuce has a substance known as lactucarium which has an effect similar to opium which has been used in sleeping draughts. Wild lettuce has a higher lactucarium content than the cultivated variety. Too much cabbage has been found to cause goitre in rabbits.

DID YOU KNOW?
In Beatrix Potter's Tale of the Flopsy Bunnies, the rabbits "simply stuffed" Mr MacGregor's lettuces and "by degrees, one after another, they were overcome with slumber, and lay down in the mown grass".

DO'S
Artichokes, corn on the cob, sweet potato, lucerne, sugar beet, radishes, swede and turnips are all acceptable. Carrot and carrot tops can be used provided they have not been sprayed for carrot fly. Strawberry leaves, raspberry canes, any fruit tree or bush prunings are excellent.

All the brassicas are valuable, such as sprouts, cauliflower, broccoli, savoy/kale and the outside leaves of cabbage. The darker the green, the better it is, as it contains more Vitamin C. Kohlrabi is also a valuable addition to the diet. Parsley is also important as it is an excellent tonic. Juniper lends flavour to rabbit feed. In the flower border, almost anything goes, including asters, marigolds, roses, chrysanthemums, carnations, sweetpeas, nasturtiums, sunflowers and mallow. These are some of the most common and are easily recognised and can be fed without fear.

DID YOU KNOW?
In a town called Lurgan, in Northern Ireland, there is a notice at the cemetery entrance: 'Do not lay wreaths of carnations, chrysanthemums or roses. The rabbits eat them'.

WILD GREENS
Before feeding your rabbits with any wild plants, you must make sure they have not been contaminated with pesticides or other chemicals. Wild green foods are not

accessible, or even recognisable, to everybody and a certain amount of knowledge is needed – although you cannot go far wrong by just cutting a great bundle from the hedgerow, for the rabbits themselves will soon sort it out.

One of the most common wild greens is the dandelion, known as Pee the Bed, or Pis-en-lit in Europe. As its name suggests, it is a pretty powerful diuretic, so feed it sparingly. Do not forget garden weeds such as groundsel and chickweed, and also shepherd's purse, which is an excellent astringent.

Both narrow-leaved and broad-leaved plantains, which are common weeds and known as 'Rats Tails', are a valuable source of protein, and the seeding stalk is much relished by caged birds. Plantains are widely available on roadsides and waste ground; the leaves grow flat at ground level and the stalk rises from the centre with a myriad of tiny green buds and seeds. As the list of such food is vast, I recommend F.R. Bell's book *Green Foods for Rabbits and Cavies*, published by *Fur and Feather*.

The nettle is very high in protein (approximately 26 per cent) and, dried off, it makes the finest hay for winter. Pick it before seeding and store it on a rack or an open-mesh sack. Never pick greenstuff, however, if the area has been sprayed. The safest place to cut green stuff is on the railway embankment – it is clean, as no dogs or cats have been roaming around the area. You would need to ask the rail company for permission first; I did and was allowed to cut up to seven miles of embankment.

There are many varieties of thistle. Sow thistle, a small, yellow-flowered thistle with grey-green leaves, also known as the milky thistle, is the most useful and is much appreciated by does in kindle. The juniper is a favourite plant with rabbits, the eating of which gives the flesh a delicate flavour.

For a detailed list of green foods, see the list of alternative green food, at the end of this chapter.

SEAWEED
Wild rabbits living on the seaboard flourish on seaweeds. I have not heard of a domestic rabbit keeper feeding it though!

GRASSES
Grasses – for the small hay patch, smooth-stalked meadow grass, also known as Kentucky Blue Grass, is ideal.
Fescue – very nutritive if cut before flowering.
Timothy or Cats tail – highly nutritive. It was introduced from the USA to the UK in 1720.
Lucerne – also useful.
Rye Grass – makes excellent hay.
Bamboo – also useful.
Millefoil or Hundred Leaf Grass – this grows anywhere and is also known as Thousand Leaf Clover. Its common name in Britain is Yarrow. Rabbits like it, and it is said to be a powerful protection against evil.

Feeding Ode For Rabbits
By G. Lodham

Do not give a Rabbit yew,
Spurge, Fool's Parsley, fever few.
Nightshade, purple or flowered white,
Lords and Ladies, Aconite.
Bryony with berries Red,
Pimpernels should not be fed.
Add Laburnum, Golden rain,
Hemlock with its Crimson stain.
Buttercup and celandine,
Foxglove, poppy and woodbine.
If they eat these, Rabbits die,
Caution says 'Don't let them try'.

ALTERNATIVE GREEN FOOD

In view of the rising cost of pellet feeding and mixes and with many enquiries about how to augment foodstuffs with green feeding, I append a more detailed list:

FEED: Avens or Geum, Agrimony, Bramble, Bindweed, Bishop Weed or Ground Elder, Burnet, Butterbur, Cow Parsnip or Hogweed, Clovers, Coltsfoot, Convolvulus, Chickweed, Goosegrass, Crosewort or Maywort, Dandelion, Dock (before seeding), Groundsel, Goutweed, Hawkweed, Heather, Hedgeparsley, Knapweed, Knotgrass, Lucerne, Mallow, Mustard, Nipplewort, Plaintain, Sea Spinach, Shepherd's Purse, Sour Dock or Sorrel, Thistles, Trefoil, Vetches or Tares, Watercress, Yarrow.

AVOID: Arum, Anemone, Deadly Nightshade, Bluebell, Buttercup, Bryony, Colchicums (Meadow Saffron), Comfrey – no longer used because it is so very rich in protein that it is now supposed to be carcinogenic, Corn Cockle, Celandine, Docks (in seed), Dog Mercury, Figwort, Foxglove, Iris, Fool's Parsley, Ground Ivy, Hemlock – easily recognised by its mousy smell and red or purple blotches on its stalk, Henbane Poppies, Scarlet Pimpernel, Spurges, Toadflax, Traveller's Joy.

CULTIVATED VEGETABLES AND ROOTS

FEED: Artichokes, Jerusalem (leaves and roots), Beetroot, Brussels Sprouts, Beans and haulm (not Scarlet Runners), Chicory, Cauliflower, Carrots, Cabbage, Celery, Clover, Dandelion, Fodder Beet, Horseradish, Kales, Kohlrabi, Lucerne, Maize, Mangolds (after December 25th), Parsley, Strawberry, late autumn Swedes, Sainfoin, Savoys, Spinach, Sunflowers, Strawberry and Raspberry leaves.

AVOID: Mangold tops, also known as Swede Turnips, Mangold roots (before December), Tomato leaves, Potato tops, Lettuce.

FLOWERS

FEED: Asters, Borage, Calendula, Centaurea, Daisies, Galega, Geranium, Geum, Helenium, Hollyhock, Honesty, Lupins (not seeds), Marguerites, Marigolds, Michaelmas Daisies, Nasturtium, Rose, Stocks, Sunflowers, Wallflowers.

AVOID: Acacia, Aconite, Antirrhinum, Arum, Anemone, Columbine, Daffodil, Dahlia, Delphinium, Feverfew, Gypsophila, Helleborus, Hyacinth, Iris, Larkspur, Lily of the Valley, Linarias, Lobelia, Love-in-a-Mist, Monkshood, Poppies, Snowdrop, Tulips and all bulbous plants.

TREES AND SHRUBS

FEED: Practically all deciduous trees, (excepting Oak leaves, very fresh growth of young leaves and twigs and green heather tips), Blackberry, Rose, Raspberry Canes.

AVOID: Most evergreen trees and shrubs, Acacia, Box, Elder, Beech masts, Gorse, acorns, seeds, Laburnum, Oak, Snowberry, Plum, Ivy (except in winter when no berries or flowers).

WARNING

- Before feeding your rabbits with any wild plants make sure they have not been contaminated with pesticides or other chemicals.
- Never feed wet or frozen green food (if in doubt, stick to rabbit pellets or a good rabbit mix).

- All clovers are now considered to be suspect, especially red clovers, because they contain dicoumerel which is an anti-coagulant (and also used in rat poison).
  Hay no longer contains a mixture of grasses and red clover, not the so sweet-smelling pink and white clover which, on a windy day, you could sniff from quite a distance away. Now just a memory!

HOMOEOPATHIC HERBS

- Blackberry or Bramble – general tonic and also helpful in pregnancy disorders. It is supposed to help in the prevention of miscarriages, as are raspberry leaves.
- Chives – general tonic and appetiser.
- Wormwood and Rue – fly repellents. Boil the leaves and then sprinkle them around problem areas.
- Pennyroyal – this is good for lungs and dust complaints. There is a tale, which I do not necessarily believe, that humans used it for abortions, so be careful.
- Tansy – a cure-all.
- Mint – supposedly good for infertility problems.
- Thyme – good for chest complaints.
- Parsley – a tonic. Bruised and steeped in vinegar it relieves mastitis.
- Rosemary – a general tonic for the reproductive system.
- Sage – increases milk flow.
- Coltsfoot – chesty colds.
- Common Willow – this contains some aspirin.

CHAPTER 5

ROUTINE CARE

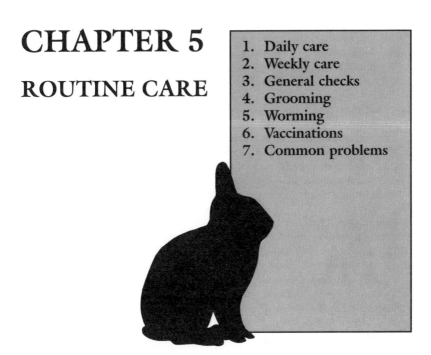

"Keep clean, feed well, lay and sleep warm."
An old Scottish farming policy for healthy stock.

All stock should be examined carefully for any signs of ill health. There is no mistaking a sick rabbit – its coat is lacklustre, its eyes are dull and it sits hunched up in a corner. The healthy rabbit is full of vigour and bounce, bright-eyed and bushy-tailed.

1. DAILY CARE

A daily routine is essential. Rabbits are creatures of habit, in many ways following in their wild ancestors' footsteps. Feeding regularly, resting during the day, and being ready to caper around in the evenings, is absolutely typical rabbit behaviour. Get your rabbit into a routine which suits you best. Always feed it at the same time each day, if possible. I always clean out the hutch corners, the toilet corners, before feeding. My rabbits can then feed and drink in peace. So remember – cleaning before feeding.

In the evenings, I possibly give them some small food treat and, of course, I top up the drinking supply. I cannot stress how important water is to *all* animals. In captivity the rabbit relies on the owner. In the wild the rabbit is self-reliant, and foraging provides all the moisture he needs. It is particularly important to check out the water supply when feeding pellets or dry mixes.

After daily cleaning, and before feeding, is a good time to check your rabbit for any signs of ill health or injuries. Settle your rabbit quietly on your lap and go over it gently from head to toe and tail. If it is inclined to be restless, lay it on its back and, with one hand clasping the back of its head, stroke it gently and lightly from under its chin down its abdomen. It will soon lie still.

When it is upturned like this you can check for any signs of vent disease, or so-called hutch burn. Lumps of muck stuck around the tail could be a sign of scouring which has dried up. Blisters and swelling of the external genitals could be due to accumulated manure and moisture in the hutch – hence the daily cleaning-out of the toilet corners. As I have written in an earlier chapter, I use gardeners' seedling trays as litter trays, but you can also use plastic washing-up bowls, the oblong ones. Layer with newspaper and then shavings. This makes it easy to empty and to clean and rabbits soon become accustomed to using a bowl. Of course, some rabbits will not do this – they prefer to use the bowl as a resting place!

All dishes must be washed daily.

2. WEEKLY CARE
All hutches should be cleaned thoroughly at least once weekly, or even twice weekly if one has a 'devil-may-care' doe. All netted doors should have fluff and dust burnt off or brushed thoroughly with disinfectant. Crisp boxes are renewed weekly, but some more frequently depending on the rabbit's teeth. The windows must be cleaned and the food bins cleaned and left secure. A more thorough weekly medical check is advisable. There is something that I do cherish and that is the cobwebs on the ceiling. There is nothing like a spider for catching a fly. If I use flypapers, I do find the more expensive ones that are used in greenhouses are actually a better buy.

3. GENERAL CHECKS

FEET
The fur on a rabbit's hind feet should be thick, like a pile carpet. Sometimes the pads have thin places in the fur, even bare patches. Short-coated rabbits such as the Rex breeds, used to be prone to bare, sore feet. Not now. The combination of good husbandry and good breeding has practically eliminated this problem. Claws should be clean and sharp, like needles. Older rabbits may need their claws clipped. Long, uncared-for nails can cause difficulties in getting about.

NAILS
Look at the rabbit's nails. They can grow quickly when soft-bedded and, in all probability, will require occasional cutting. This is simply done with a good pair of nail clippers. Tuck the rabbit under your arm and examine the nail – the blood vessel is easily seen, so simply cut off the dead end. Turn the rabbit over, still holding it firmly under your arm and do the back nails. Easier still, sit the rabbit on its rump, grasp the loose skin on the back, just below the nape of the neck, and get to work. You will soon get the hang of it!

EARS
Check ears for wax or mites or any sign of scratching. They should be clear and pink all the way down. Any signs of discharge or brown scabs may be a sign of ear canker.

Particular care should be taken wih Lop-eared rabbits.

TEETH
Check your rabbit's teeth to see that they are properly aligned. The normal bite of a rabbit's teeth has the upper incisors overlapping the bottom ones. Malocclusion, which is also known as buck teeth or wolf teeth, means that the lower incisors are in front of the upper incisors, and that they are usually over-long and sometimes curving to the sides. The problem seems to be getting more prevalent. It can be a hereditary fault in breeding, or is a genetic recessive. This is controversial. Parents who carry the recessive gene, although they themselves have normal teeth, have an up to 25 per cent chance of their offspring having the defect. Malocclusion can also result from injury by biting and pulling on the hutch or the cage wire. Most rabbit breeders cull stock with malocclusion, but there are pet shop breeders who may not do this, and then the defect is passed on. Testing parents by, for example, breeding the buck back to his daughter, will show whether the rabbits are carrying this trait.

EYES
These should be clear, bright and free from discharge. Check the eyelashes as well. An ingrown eyelash can cause problems. The so-called weepy eyes often occur in bucks when hutches have been allowed to become saturated with ammoniac urine.

NOSE
The fur around the rabbit's nose should have a shiny, silky appearance. If there is any wetness around the nose or on the insides of the front paws, the rabbit should be isolated. It may be just a cold (coryza) or the beginning of something more serious (Pasteurella). Do be aware that rabbits wipe their noses with the insides of their front paws.

4. GROOMING
Healthy rabbits need very little grooming. Moult is sometimes a problem, especially in fur breeds, but remember that moult is a natural process and not a disease – it is simply the death of old hair and the re-growth of new hair.

A rabbit will soon learn to accept grooming.   *The long coated breeds need more attention.*

For flat-coated rabbits a good rub with a piece of sheep's wool is excellent and it also gives a terrific shine. Sheep's wool is easily come by if you live in the country as you can find masses of it stuck on fences. All that is needed is a quick swish in soapy water to clean the wool and then to let it dry. It will still retain a certain amount of oil which adds to the shine. Wool from the black-faced sheep is ideal, being rougher and tougher. This type of wool is normally used for all wool carpets. If this is not available, a soft brush will do. Polish the fur with a piece of silk. Do not use hairdressing toiletries, especially on an exhibition rabbit – and **never** use bleach on white rabbits! Angora rabbits need a different type of grooming, which is dealt with in a later chapter.

A raw, peeled potato is excellent for cleaning dirty feet, or commercially-produced face wipes are good as an emergency cleaner.

5. WORMING

Rabbits are remarkably free from such parasites; particularly those fed on pellets are highly unlikely to become infested with worms. Occasionally, rabbits fed with greenstuff can catch tapeworm from food contaminated by dogs. I do, however, know of very fussy breeders who routinely dose their rabbits for tapeworms and threadworms, using a children's dose for the latter.

6. VACCINATIONS

Rabbits can be vaccinated against myxomatosis, and haemorrhagic viral disease and there is an anti-fertility vaccine intended to limit the numbers of wild rabbits. These vaccines are administered twice yearly. Research is going on to find a vaccine for mucoid enteritis.

7. COMMON PROBLEMS

There are some common faults which can lead to ill health, and, in many cases, these can be prevented.

Problems with stock
- Badly-reared youngsters.
- Purchase of cheap rabbits from unknown sources.
- Stock weaned too early.

Housing Problems
- Overcrowding.
- Inadequate bedding.
- Dirty housing, feeding dishes or drinking bottles.
- Poor ventilation.
- Inadequate protection from the weather.

Feeding Faults
- Feeding mouldy, fermenting foodstuffs.
- Overfeeding.
- Underfeeding.
- Irregular feeding.
- Feeding of dangerous plants.
- Feeding new hay.

Infectious Diseases
- Failure to note early signs of ill health, for example, scouring, scratching, sneezing, dull coat, running eyes.
- Failure to isolate sick stock.
- Handling healthy animals after diseased one without washing your hands thoroughly.

External Disturbances
- Rats, mice, strangers, dogs, cats, stoats etc. can lead to panic and stress.

Physical Injury
There is a variety of causes, for example:
- Careless and inexpert handling by owner or by judge or stewards at shows.
- Bites from other rabbits.
- Protruding nails in hutches.
- Torn wire netting.
- Chipped food dishes.

Poisoning
- Injudicious use of fly-sprays or creosoted wood or lead paint. (Remember that the rabbit is an expert at gnawing wood). There are non-poisonous fly-sprays available, which are the ones you should use.

CHAPTER 6

THE HOUSE RABBIT

"We went out for the day, and when we came home,
Buttercup had completely demolished a wicker chair."
From an old rabbit book, dated 1814, entitled *Rabbit Keeping* by Delamer.

Any rabbit can be a house rabbit, for a house rabbit is simply a rabbit that has been trained to live inside its owner's home. The practice is not new, far from it. Louis XIV had a pet rabbit, and Napoleon III kept a rabbit when in prison. It was from this experience that his idea of the allotment of rabbits to smallholders was born (see Chapter One). The Russian revolutionary Trotsky also kept a white rabbit.

John Lawrence wrote about rabbits around the end of 1799. In one chapter headed 'Mad, Tame Conies', he wrote: "The rabbit is a caressing animal and equally fond, with the cat, of having its head stroked. At the same time, it is not destitute of courage".

He also wrote of a "whimsical lady" who admitted a buck rabbit into her house where he became her companion for 12 months. He soon intimidated the cats so much, by chasing them all round the house, darting on them and tearing their hair off in mouthfuls, that they very seldom dared to approach. He slept in her lap by choice, or upon the most comfortable chair or the hearthrug. He was as full of tricks and mischief as a monkey. He destroyed a whole set of rush-bottomed chairs and would refuse nothing to eat or drink that had been eaten or drunk by any other member of the family!

1. THE PROS AND CONS

The House Rabbit Society was founded in California in 1988, and it has flourished and has grown over the last 10 years from 300 to 7,000 members in the USA. It is a non-profit-making animal welfare organisation with a twofold mission:

• To rescue abandoned rabbits and find them permanent homes through adoption.
• To educate the owners, thereby improving the life of the rabbit, and helping people to understand these often misunderstood 'companion' animals.

Since the society was founded, over 5,500 rabbits have been rescued. The Society is a volunteer organisation with terrific publicity know-how. The idea spread to the UK and this newest recruit to the House Rabbit Society, the British House Rabbit Association, has had an outstanding success, and again publicity is spot-on. Its membership has now outstripped that of the National Rabbit Council.

The House Rabbit Society believes that all rabbits are valuable as individuals, regardless of breed purity, state of health or relationship to humans. The welfare of all rabbits is their primary consideration. This I heartily endorse. They state: "It is in the best interests of wild rabbits that human intervention be held to a minimum except where the wild ones are sick, being nursed or rehabilitated. Domestic rabbits are not the product of natural selection but rather of human interference with breeding programmes etc. It is therefore a human responsibility to see that these animals be cared for. Domestic rabbits are companion animals and should be afforded the same individual rights, care, and opportunity for longevity as is commonly afforded to cats and dogs which live as human companions."

It must be remembered that there is a vast difference between rabbits and cats and dogs. The first is a prey animal, whereas cats and dogs are natural predators; also, the rabbit was not really domesticated until the late 19th century, whereas dogs and cats have been domesticated for many centuries. To keep a rabbit in the house means that they become like lap dogs. Also they are robbed of their sex because they have to be neutered to keep them from spraying. Castration is a fairly simple surgical operation and recovery is swift. It is usually carried out when the buck is between four and six months of age. There is also chemical castration, where an injection of 0.2 mm of calcium chloride solution is put into the bottom of each testicle. This causes the testicles to dry up in about 10 days.

Spaying a female rabbit is slightly more difficult. The British House Rabbit Association states that it is not yet routine in the UK and an owner must be prepared to travel to find a vet experienced at spaying.

If you do decide to have a home rabbit, it is better to have a buck. Not only are they cheaper and easier to castrate than does, they also become more amenable and easier to handle.

It is also worth remembering that the house rabbit is being subjected to a new environment with different bacteria and possibly harmful viruses, as well as housemites. It must be pointed out that it is not only the rabbit that is vulnerable to potential danger from its new house environment; humans run a risk of disease by their close proximity to a house rabbit. Tuleraemia is one such disease and it can be fatal. Risks also include an allergic reaction to fur, and flu-like symptoms within 10 days of receiving a deep scratch or a bite.

2. RABBIT-PROOFING YOUR HOME
The old Scottish doggerel or rabbit grace could equally apply to the house rabbit:

Up wae yer head
Doon wae yer paws
And thank the Lord
For a guid pour of jaws

Rabbits need to gnaw – and this can pose a considerable problem when they are placed in a domestic environment. Potential hazards come from trailing electrical cables, and the possible damage to furniture is enormous. The UK House Rabbit Association has come up with ideas to prevent the demolition of furniture and covers. It suggests giving your rabbit lots of chewable toys, such as loo roll inners and cardboard boxes, and being on the alert, so that when it tries to chew a forbidden object, it can be distracted by one of the toys. It also suggests that cables and flexes should be covered or hung up on walls. Many owners of house rabbits confine their pet to one room of the house, and this means that this area can be completely rabbit-proof.

An electrical insurance company has reported that the antics of house rabbits are causing increased damage to electrical equipment and costing householders hundreds of pounds in replacement or repair costs.

House rabbits that are nervous and inclined to wreck the house may be suffering from a lack of Vitamin B, which can be treated by the addition of a supplement sprinkled on the food ration. There are various sprays for carpets and curtains which repel cats and dogs, and will probably work on rabbits, too. Always check the label before use, and, if necessary, consult a vet.

Potted plants can also constitute a danger. My rabbit, Sooty, demolished a whole windowsill of potted geraniums with no harm done except the loss of some very good plants, but it could easily have been different. Many potted plants are harmful, and indeed poisonous, both to the owner and to the house rabbit.

The following plants are very poisonous and harmful if eaten by house pets:

Dieffenbachia	Leopard Lily
Hedera	Ivy – any variety
Pink Jasmine	Solanum
Senecio	String of Beads
Tradescantia	Wandering Jew aka Wandering Sailor
Primula Obconica	Poison Primrose
Primula	Fairy Primrose
Poinsettia	Winter Cherry
Cineraria	Devil's Ivy
Miltonia	Swiss Cheese Plant
Pothos	Daffodils, Hyacinths, any bulb plant.

3. HOUSE-TRAINING
One good thing about house rabbits is that they are easily trained to use a litter box or tray. Even rabbits in the wild never soil their homes. Rabbits in hutches always use the same corner, so you can watch where the rabbit

goes in the house and then put the litter tray there. The rabbit will quickly catch on. Alternatively, it is recommended that you start your house rabbit off by putting it in a cage in the home and then gradually extending the free-range time. Indoor cages are now available. Put the litter tray in the cage with the rabbit and shut the rabbit in until it is using its litter tray correctly. Then you can start letting it out. Do respect its territory and let it come to you, do not invade its cage.

I do have a word of warning about litter trays. Recently there was a near disaster where cat litter of the absorbent clay type was used. The owner went on holiday leaving the rabbits in an outdoor hutch. A friend who was asked to keep an eye on them failed to appear for two or three days. The poor rabbits began to eat the litter, which expanded in the digestive tract and then became completely compacted. Fortunately, a neighbour saw their distress and called the vet. After an enema and a suppository they recovered. It is preferable to use wood-based cat litter for the litter tray.

4. EXERCISE
House rabbits need plenty of exercise and should be allowed some free-running – a staircase makes an excellent gym! They should never be let outside without supervision, and if you keep a cat make sure your rabbit does not try the cat flap. I know of one owner who kept a house rabbit, a doe, who discovered the cat flap and went walkabout. She came home next morning, via the cat flap, and the owner welcomed her with caresses and praise. Four weeks later the owner was horrified to find her pet had become the mother of five half-wild babies.

House rabbits also need toys to play with. They love demolishing small cardboard boxes and play for hours pushing soft-drinks cans around. An American idea is to push a marble through the opening of the can. Rabbits love to play with that.

5. HARNESS TRAINING
Some rabbits, like some cats, can be trained to wear a harness, or a collar with a lead. Try using one that has been designed for a cat. Start by just putting the collar on and let the rabbit get used to that. Then attach the lead. Be very careful, however, that you are not making the rabbit vulnerable by restricting it in this way and leaving it at the mercy of an aggressive dog or cat.

> *DID YOU KNOW?*
> *Some years ago, an Edinburgh lady was evicted from her house for growing a lawn in her front room for the rabbits that she kept there.*

6. ROUTINE CARE
The feeding of house rabbits is no different to the feeding of other domestic rabbits; that is, they should be fed once daily with pellets, hay, fresh vegetables and water. Grooming is simply a daily brushing and combing. A flea collar might also be a good idea. You will also need to buy a suitable indoor hutch (see Chapter Three).

7. SEEKING ADVICE
No matter where you live, advice is readily available. Both the UK House Rabbit Association and the USA House Rabbit Society are to be found on the Internet, and their addresses can be found in the Appendices.

CHAPTER 7

BREEDING RABBITS

The first rule of caring for breeding stock is a saying of Moses: *"Thou shalt not let thy cattle gender with a diverse kind"*. If you do, you end up producing mongrels. The second rule to remember is: *Vigorous parents produce vigorous litters.*

1. THE BUCK

The buck is the most important member of the rabbitry. He must be in the best of condition if he is to reproduce lively, vigorous stock of good type, good bones and ones that are, of course, fertile. He should have his own roomy hutch and be exercised two to three times a week. A well-exercised buck is worth much more than one who gets no exercise. Bucks should not be used until they are fully adult and in full adult coat, which is at roughly six to eight months.

Rabbits are normally resting during the daytime and most active at night and, therefore, it is easier at the beginning or end of the day to put the doe to the buck. Also, according to work done at Bristol University researching fertility, the buck produces a higher sperm count in the early morning, which lessens as the day progresses. It is not a good idea to leave the doe overnight with the buck because a too-vigorous buck will indulge in a number of unnecessary matings.

In Switzerland every three years there is the 'Great All-Buck Show'. There you will find over 6,000 bucks exhibited from all over Europe. The breeders plan their breeding from one buck show to the next, producing some of the finest stock in the world.

40

2. THE DOE

The doe should also be of good type, in sound health and in full adult coat when mated for the first time. Never mate when the doe is in moult, and ensure that she is in season before mating. The doe should be put to the buck in his hutch, not the other way round. If the doe is not in season she can be put to the buck for a short time each day until she accepts him, although it is unwise to force mating. Does which will accept the buck often show a congested moist vagina with a reddish coloration.

Three to four litters per year is enough for a valuable doe. Exhibiting breeders chasing Championships ('pot-hunting') usually mate their does in time to have a young adult fit to show.

Does have a wonderful means of birth control. If an insufficient number of eggs have been fertilised, they are re-absorbed and the doe comes into season again quickly, without wasting time just to produce one or two babies. If, on the other hand, a large number of eggs have been fertilised, and the doe is not feeling 'in the pink' or there is insufficient feeding, she will re-absorb the surplus and produce what is the natural or ideal number – usually four to five youngsters.

3. THE LITTER

The pregnant doe should have a larger hutch which is roomy and comfortable, as youngsters must have room to develop. From the day of mating, the doe should be well fed and have plenty of water and milk to drink. The gestation period is 28-31 days. A nest box should be provided, with the side of the box just high enough to allow the doe access, but to keep the youngsters in. The doe should also be furnished with plenty of soft nesting material, meadow hay or finely shredded paper, or dried moss. Some breeders keep the fur from former nests to augment the new nest. In cooler weather a polystyrene tile slipped under the nest box will give added warmth.

After the birth, the nest of youngsters should be left alone and the babies not touched. After a day or so, gently part the nesting material for inspection. If all is well leave well alone for at least five days.

First-litter does often fail to make a nest and have the litter on the hutch floor. If noticed early, the youngsters can be retrieved by the breeder. Rabbits, unlike cats, cannot retrieve their own kits so, unless they are picked up by the breeder, the baby rabbits will die. The doe's milk may take 24 hours or more to flow. If she is reluctant to feed the babies, take them all to a warm place, lay the doe on your lap with teats uppermost, and try attaching the youngsters to the teats. This can work and will aid the milk flow.

Sometimes, for various reasons, the doe may desert her litter completely or scatter them all over the hutch. If found early enough, the youngsters can be collected and put into a box lined with warm material and kept in a warm place for 24 hours. For the first few hours of their lives they can exist without milk, but they cannot live without warmth!

The most common cause of a doe's neglect is that the milk flow has not begun. If the milk flow starts within a few hours of birth, as it often does, the youngsters can be returned to the nest. It is important not to handle the babies, but if it is really necessary, then rub your hands over the doe's fur first, for this will transfer her odour to the babies.

If the doe is a good mother, and has made a snug nest, do not disturb it. Make sure the new litter does not come into contact with the cold sides of the box. Some breeders advise limiting the number of babies in the nest in the hope of giving the remainder a good start in life; this is not a good idea – the doe is well able to deal with her litter. For the first three weeks, the litter exists solely on the mother's milk which is three times more nutritious than that of a cow. The babies are fed by the doe once daily. The composition of the doe's milk is as follows: 15 per cent protein, 10 per cent fat, 2 per cent sugar, and 3 per cent minerals – the rest is water.

4. WEANING

From 16 to 21 days, the youngsters begin to eat pellets, rabbit mix and hay in increasing amounts. Too much fibre should be avoided; protein is all-important and fresh water should always be available. Some firms produce food pellets for nursing does and for weaners

At six to eight weeks the doe should be removed to another hutch, preferably one next to the family. Personally, I leave the litter with the doe for as long as she can tolerate them – usually two months. However, I segregate the young bucks. Exhibition stock should be ringed with a Rabbit Association identity ring at this time.

From the time of weaning, the growing youngsters should be allowed to eat as much as they can, but any changes in diet or quantity should be done gradually to avoid tummy upsets.

5. SEXING

Sexing your rabbit leaves room for making some bloomers. I have entered a young buck in a doe class and vice versa – and have never lived it down. It can be very difficult to sex very young rabbits (under four months) although the buck ought to be easy to check by the testes. The doe's vulva is narrower and closer to the anal opening than the penis of the buck. Other differences can be noted in the type of head; for instance, the buck's is broader than that of the doe which is much finer. It should be fairly easy to sex your rabbits at eight weeks. (See illustration).

6. TROUBLE-SHOOTING

Being a breeder can also be a stressful affair. Many worries can arise in the course of breeding your rabbits, and it is always better to be aware of potential trouble, and try to intervene before problems arise.

PROBLEM CHECKLIST
- Barking dogs.
- Hungry cats on the prowl.
- Sudden loud noises.
- The hutch door is left open.
- Chewed hutch walls or cage wire.
- Broken locks.
- Nosy/noisy children.

7. COMMERCIAL RABBIT BREEDING

Being a member of the breeding and exhibiting of show rabbits fraternity should not blind one to the other aspects of rabbit breeding. There is much to be learned from the commercial breeder.

As I mentioned at the beginning of this book, commercial breeding goes back a very long way before anyone dreamed of exhibition shows for rabbits. The Romans began it by making walled gardens and enclosing rabbits in them for food consumption. The monks carried it further and were more selective. After the monks came the Warreners.

Warreners were widely spread all over England, producing tons of meat and pelts. At the beginning of the 18th century, the warrener began enclosing his warrens, first by wooden palings, then by stone walls and then by walls of grass sods. The sods were 16 x 12 ins, laid one on top of the other. The top of the wall was capped by reeds, blackthorn and blackberry. You can still see reminders of these walls even now if you look closely enough when in warren country. These walls had an estimated life of seven years. They were not escape-proof, however, and by the 19th century many farmers were netting the insides and tops of the walls. The rabbit farmers of this time had two aims: to breed as many rabbits as possible and to produce meat of the highest quality.

Food supplies for the stock were kept up by cropping various wild plants such as thistles, dandelions, groundsel, and parsley, and a haystack was placed in the middle of the compound. Turnips were fed in winter but breeders found that an all-turnip diet gave them pot-bellied rabbits. The normal ratio was 1 buck to 10 does, although one Norfolk breeder thought that 1 buck to 4 does was better because it ensured a well-balanced colony in a breeding season. A colony of 100 pairs could clear an annual profit that would have been a handsome sum in those days. Transport costs, however, were high.

8. THE FIRST INDOOR RABBITRIES
The first mention of indoor rabbitries is described a book published in around 1799 which mentions stock housed in a boarded shed. There were at that time two commercial rabbit feeders (not breeders), one in Oxfordshire and one in Berkshire, having 500-2000 breeding does each. These were housed in huts and were generally placed one above the other to the height required.

Where a large stock was kept, the hutches were placed in rows with sufficient space between for feeding and cleaning instead of being joined to the wall. It was preferable to rest the hutches on stands about a foot above ground for convenience in cleaning underneath. Each hutch intended for breeding had two rooms – a feeding room and a bedroom with a sliding door between the two for confining the rabbit during cleaning. There were single hutches for weaned rabbits and bucks, which had to be kept separate. The rabbit house would stand on a dry foundation and be well ventilated. Exposure to too much humidity was fatal to the rabbits.

The rabbit house also contained a tub for dung and a bin to contain one day's supply of food. So, in almost 200 years the basic rules have changed but little. In that early farming of rabbits, does were mated at six months and mated again six weeks later after kindling. They had an average of five litters per year – an estimated 2,000 young from 100 does. The rabbits were generally sold from 'the teat'. There is a table of figures of the number of rabbits sold between October and March, which was given to the Select Committee of the House of Commons in 1873, when the game laws were in question, by a game dealer in Manchester:

Liverpool	500,000
Manchester	500,000
Birmingham	350,000
The Potteries	300,000
Nottingham	200,000
Leeds, Newcastle and Sheffield	150,000

Each week 1,000 rabbits were sold in Chester. These were sold, skinned, weighing 1lb to 2 lb at an average price of three to five shillings per dozen. It was at least six pence per pound cheaper than any other meat.

Of course there was terrific competition from Europe. In the mid-1880s, Belgium was exporting 26,000,000 rabbits per year to Britain. It is also very odd to discover that in 1900 New Zealand and Australia were exporting tinned rabbit to Britain.

In the last War, Australia was sending huge consignments of tinned rabbit to the US Army in the South Pacific Islands. One day a piece of fur was found in a tin and the US Army sent back the consignment to Australia which, in turn, sold it to the British Army. No doubt this was the meat in the notorious 'Meat and Veg' fed to the Army in the various campaigns, although I must admit I never found any fluff in my meals. The flavour of the tinned wartime rabbit was pronounced as being 'too sweet' – not like the wild ones, but rather like the difference between field and cultivated mushrooms.

Between the wars, skins were in great demand. Although any white rabbit could be dyed or imprinted to represent other animals, leopard, tiger, ocelot etc., rabbits were bred to make their pelts resemble other valuable mammal skins such as the chinchilla, silver fox, sable and ermine, and even the humble agouti was not forgotten. Fur breeds were valuable, but now they have declined in numbers and the Dwarf breeds have taken over, possibly because of rising food costs.

The domestic rabbit could become a great meat species especially for poorer countries. They can be housed on almost anything. They can convert forage into meat more successfully than cattle, and more cheaply too. Also, the skins are in fair demand for toy-making, although market values do fluctuate. Today, the poacher has long since ceased to ply his trade and, after the problems of myxomatosis and other such diseases, the demand for commercially-bred rabbits has fallen considerably. There appear to be two exceptions to this – the meat pet trade, and packaged pieces of frozen rabbit in the supermarkets, almost on a par with the cost of beef.

Rabbit farming in the UK has fallen since the war years and today's suppliers are mostly European or Chinese. Even the fur trade has hit rock bottom, as fashion was fickle and animal liberators were rife.

9. JUDGING COMMERCIAL RABBITS

I used to be a member of the Commercial Rabbit Association, not because I wanted to be a rabbit farmer (far from it), but because I was interested in seeing the opposite side of the coin. I would never make a commercial rabbit farmer as I cannot kill a rabbit, nor skin it, nor eat it! I did, however, judge some commercial classes (although I had to get another breeder to produce the carcasses for judging) and I give the standards here because sometimes a class for commercial rabbits turns up at Agricultural Shows.

DOES AND LITTERS

Doe		
Conformation and health	=	60 pts
Milking	=	20 pt
Evenness and Weight	=	20 pts
		100 pts
Litters age 3-6 weeks		
Type and Conformation	=	60 pts
Condition	=	20 pts
Evenness of Weight	=	20 pts
		100 pts
Breeding Trio (this consists of 1 buck and 2 does)		
Conformation	=	70 pts
Health	=	20 pts
Cleanliness	=	10 pts
		100 pts
Stud Buck		
Conformation	=	70 pts
Health	=	20 pts
Cleanliness	=	10 pts
		100 pts

When judging a doe and litter, look at the family before beginning; if the litter has, for example, five youngsters and two are huddled in another corner, then they may have been added to the original litter. At four weeks, young rabbits should be active and quite lively. The doe should be examined to see if she still has milk and that her teats are healthy, in fact she should be in perfect health. The litter scores where there are more does than bucks, as does are seen as 'the producers'. All the rabbits should be examined thoroughly and must be in good health. The carcasses are judged for weight and quality of meat. There should, of course, be no signs of any disease.

The most popular of all commercial breeds is the American New Zealand White, which has great conformation and a beautiful pelt. This rabbit was introduced into Britain in the 1930s, appearing both on the show bench and in rabbit farms. It is now found all over the world, particularly where farming is concerned. Its wonderful type has suffered some loss as a result of breeders not being content to leave well alone after it was accepted as a show rabbit, and the emphasis is now on its fur quality. The Californian rabbit runs a close second to the New Zealand White and is also widely known. The creator recognised that a meat rabbit with a good commercial type of pelt would be very useful and it has very good type indeed with fine bone. Both are good breeders and good mothers.

I have seen several commercial rabbit farms abroad, from the high-tech type, run by computer, to the small one-man outfits. One I saw had a row of hutches with an entrance hole at the back for the buck, who was confined to the buck corridor behind the hutches. He was free to go where he pleased, while all the does wore little plastic collars which prevented them from entering the buck corridor. The owner expected 10 litters per year from each doe. Most large commercial rabbitries are brick and concrete, with cages slung over long, deep troughs. These cages are well away from the walls to make cleaning easy, and some of the houses have roofs which can be raised or lowered depending on weather and temperature, with ventilation bricks placed along the outside walls nearer the ground.

10. WORM FARMING

A very lucrative sideline operated by commercial breeders was the introduction of worm farming on the rabbit manure. Pellet dust, in fact anything such as lawn clippings, hay, leaves etc. can make a huge compost heap for such farming (but not in the rabbitry!). An earthworm working the surface at night and boring into the earth by day will cast up its weight in fresh soil every 24 hours. These castings make exceptional plant food. The earthworm has been found to be extremely rich in nitrogen and potash. Farmers, gardeners and fishermen will buy the worms – the first two for the benefit of good pasture, the second for his fruit, vegetables and plants, and the third for the pleasure of catching fish (the Brandling is the best worm for fishing). The Brandling worm is large and breeds quickly and can be bred in drainage ducts with a rough gravel base and rabbit droppings. This base should be roughly 30 cms (12 ins) deep, kept moist, and kept at a temperature between 5 and 21 degrees Centigrade.

Other clients will include game breeders and fish hatcheries. One earthworm produces 1000 more per year. Worms being sold can be sent out in waxed containers with holes in the lids. These containers can then be enclosed in a cardboard box (also with ventilation holes) and packed in damp peat moss.

11. ANGORA FARMING

The Angora Rabbit is world-famous for its fine, silky wool which lends itself to being mixed with other types of thread such as linen or silk; therefore breeding Angoras is a different sort of commercial activity. Angora farming on a large scale is not common in the UK and we have only one Angora farm in Scotland. China was one of the largest exporters of Angora wool, until the calcivirus or VHD struck, causing the loss of 45,000 Angoras in 1988. It was a double loss, for the Angora was also a meat rabbit.

The first major account of a rabbit with a long coat was in 1708 and was found in an English rabbit book *The Whole Art of Husbandry*. The author, Mortimer, makes mention of a 'white shock Turkey Rabbet', which could be translated as the white Turkish Rabbit with long hair. After this it was known as the Rabbit of Angora. Under this name it appears in the Encyclopaedia of 1765 and was described in 1800 by Valmont de Bomare in his *Dictionaire Universal de l'Histoire Naturelles*.

The name Angora then became synonymous with 'long hair' and the rabbit fitting this description was known as the Angora rabbit of England in the 18th century (although it is more than likely that the English used the Angora's wool towards the end of the 17th century). The sale of live Angoras was forbidden in England and penalties were severe (a gruesome description can be found in Christopher Hibbert's *The Roots of Evil, A Social History of Crime and Punishment,* Penguin 1963).

In 1777, Von Meyerbach introduced some Angoras into Germany and, in 1789, a book was published in Dresden by F. Mayer on *The Breeding of the Angora Rabbit or English Rabbit.* In France, in the *Presse Industrielle* of May 1797, we learn that Angora wool was spun and that the Empress Catherine II of Russia said she was pleased to have a pair of wool stockings so soft and warm. In 1856 the Compte d'Empresmenil, Secretary of the Société Imperiale d'Acclimatation, visited an establishment concerned with the breeding of Angora rabbits at St Innocent, near Aix-les-Bains, and saw many Angora rabbits of all colours bred in colonies. The wool was plucked four times a year and he stated that "this wool, spun into fine thread, is used to make baby clothes which are sold for almost 30 Francs". Four years later, Mariot-Didieux gave details of the breeding establishments at St Innocent in his guide on breeding these rabbits.

In 1840, farming of the Angora was well developed in Savoy, France – the breeders being M and Mme Lard. Mme Lard's niece produced gloves, stockings, knee covers and various bits and pieces for rheumatic knees etc. There were also garments for the frail and delicate. The Lards also confirmed that Angora wool was often mixed with silk (in 1904, the Angora was often referred to as the "silk rabbit").

Angora farming spread all over France and, in 1930, Nantes won an award from the Chamber of Commerce for the important part the area played in exporting the wool to Britain and USA. In the Second World War, the Angora wool industry declined as it was not really essential to the war effort and in 1945 it was estimated that there were around 200,000 Angora rabbits scattered all over the country in more than 10,000 rabbitries. France was producing 90 tonnes annually, which was almost 90 per cent of the world's output.

After the war ended, breeders looked more to Angora wool production and, by 1953, 1 kilo of Angora wool fetched large sums, although it was a highly speculative market which was subject to swinging highs and lows.

Various Boards to regulate the Angora came and went until, finally, the present Syndicate of Angora Breeders was formed. This body was responsible for bringing together all the different bodies under one umbrella, thus allowing the continuation of breeding during the difficult years when output of wool dropped to around 65-70 tonnes. Now it has risen once again in the last decade to 100 tonnes of wool and hopefully the depression of the years of the mid-1970s until the end of the 1980s has gone.

In Britain, the Angora is confined to the very dedicated body of craftswomen and men who not only exhibit but spin, knit and sell the most exquisite garments. They are a scattered lot, from Lands End to the outer isles of Orkney and Shetland. They not only spin their wool but also do their own dyeing using various plants. Every year, they produce a most interesting yearbook with all articles contributed by club members. There are some really good books on Angora breeding and management, which is a specialised subject.

Recently, the French and German Angora types have been imported into the UK and I only hope that we do not lose the wonderful English Angora, with its long, fine wool, with outcrosses to the European. Certainly the latter produces more wool per year but it is of a different texture – the coat is more dense and the hair staples are not so long.

With regard to colour, in the 19th century there were three colours: white, brown and grey, the latter being a mixture of black and white, and the white being the best known. Now we have several colours, although white remains the most popular as it can be dyed to any colour.

It is interesting to note that American Angora breeders have created a Satin-coated Angora with a finer wool than any other Angora, so that it appears less dense in coat. It has three types of hair, or underwool, with an intermediate strong, wiry wool that is longer than the underwool. The guard hairs are strong and straight and protrude over the in-between fleece.

I am not a spinner, nor even an Angora breeder, but I have found the following note of great interest on spinning Angora wool – a simple spindle can be made by sticking a knitting needle through a halved potato.

12. DYEING CLOTH

Dyes are very old. It is not known when they were first used. The earliest were most likely to be stains rather than dyes. In ancient Eygpt, cloths were dyed in many lovely colours which came mostly from herbs and roots, berries, nuts and lichens etc. The Bible tells us about the Israelites who dyed ram skins red, and also about Joseph's coat of many colours. The Phoenicians made a purple dye from crushed mollusc shells and this dye was being made 15 centuries before Christ.

Scarlet was the colour for war. This dye was made from an insect which lived on oak and holly leaves. In America it was soon found that the cochineal insect was a very good source of this dye. Dyes made from old plants include indigo which has been used for over 3,000 years.

A mordant was a substance which had to be mixed with the colouring matter to fix the colour on cloths. Mordants also produce different shades with the same dye stuff. All sorts of things were used as mordants – extracts of leaves and roots, alum, iron, tin. Today there are about 3,000 different synthetic dyes.

SOME DYES

Sandalwood chips. These came from Tasmania. They need no preparation. The mordant is alum. The chips and the alum are mixed and then left for 30 minutes. At this point, the dye bath is halved. In one half add vinegar which gives a wine-red colour. To the other half, add baking soda, which gives a good blue. Note: Sandalwood obtained in UK did not react to baking soda.
Onion skins give yellow with alum – deep gold with chrome mordants.
Dahlia flowers – lemon to brown or green depending on mordants used.
Alum – gives lemon, chrome = gold.
Iron – brown green.
Tin – orange.
Red rose petals give a nice green with alum. Other plant materials to use include nettles, dandelion heads, marigolds, yellow bedstraw (roots).

NOTE:

Alum = potassium aluminium sulphate.
Chrome = potassium dichromate.
Iron = ferrous sulphate.
Tin = stanous chloride.
All mordants are poisonous. Do not use any equipment that you would subsequently use in the kitchen.

The hooded rabbit.
From the British
Museum, c.1791.

Tri-coloured rabbit:
Forerunner of all
tricolour breeds.
c.1894.

Havanna.
From the Whippell
Collection,
reproduced from
Fur & Feather,
1927.

HOUSING RABBITS

The rabbit hutch should be as big as possible. It should be located in a draught-free area, and must be well ventilated.

The rabbit cage is used for the house rabbit.

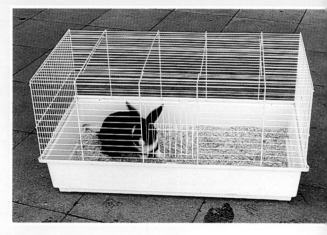

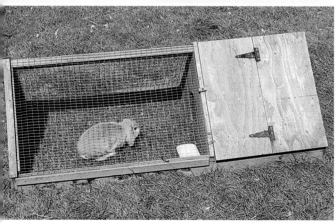

A run, with a shaded area, will be much appreciated.

Feeding the correct diet is probably the most important aspect of rabbit keeping.

Pellets are scientifically compounded to give the correct nutritional balance.

Check for quality and freshness before buying a rabbit mix.

Hay should have been cut for six months before feeding to rabbits.

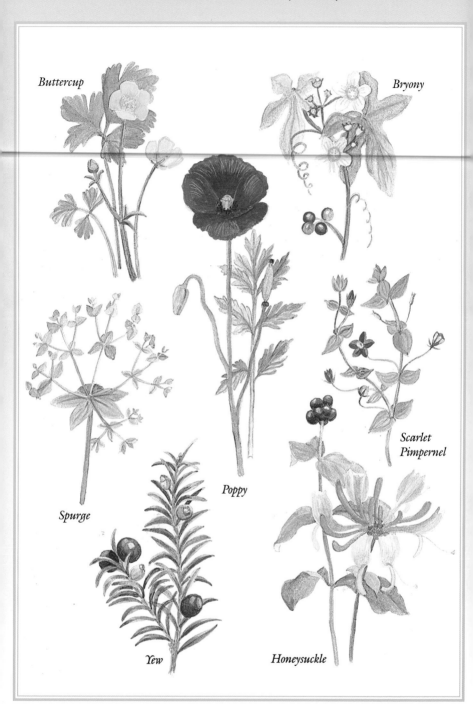

Buttercup

Bryony

Spurge

Poppy

Scarlet
Pimpernel

Yew

Honeysuckle

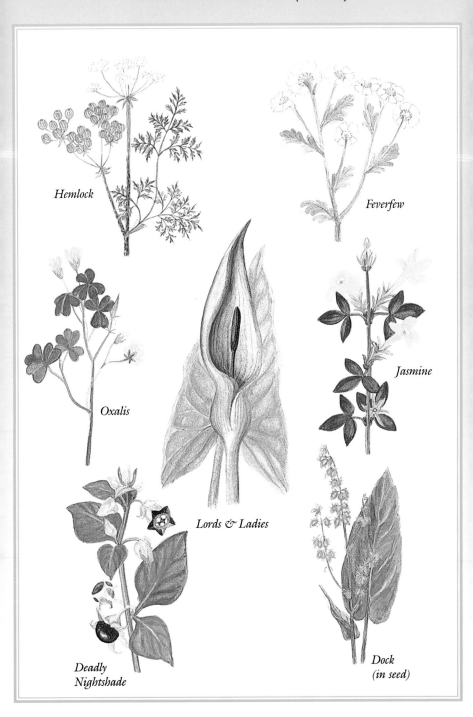

Hemlock

Feverfew

Oxalis

Jasmine

Lords & Ladies

Deadly
Nightshade

Dock
(in seed)

POISONOUS PLANTS (HOUSE)

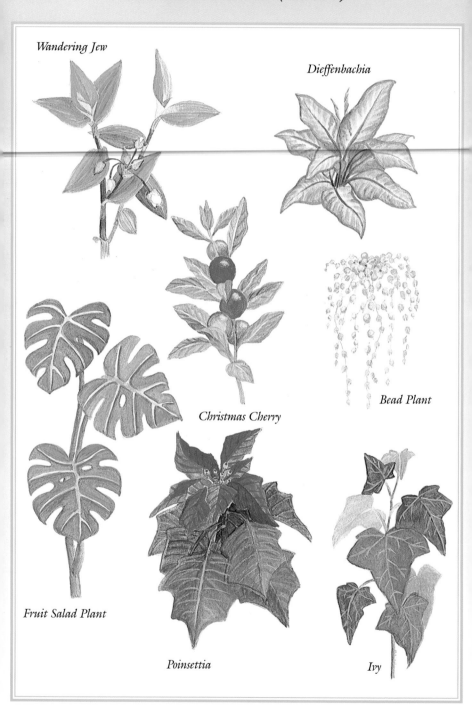

Wandering Jew

Dieffenbachia

Christmas Cherry

Bead Plant

Fruit Salad Plant

Poinsettia

Ivy

 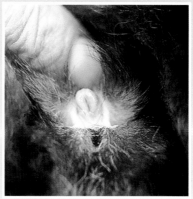

Male. *Female.*

Newborn Dwarf Lop.

One week old.

BREEDING RABBITS

Ten days old.

Three weeks old.

Six weeks old.

SECTION II: HEALTH CARE

CHAPTER 8

ANATOMY AND PHYSIOLOGY

1. The skeleton
2. The teeth
3. The digestive system
4. The respiratory system
5. The cardiovascular system
6. The sense organs
7. The urinary system
8. The reproductive system
9. The skin and scent marking glands

1. THE SKELETON

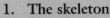

The rabbit has a delicate skeleton compared with other mammals. It makes up only 8 per cent of the rabbit's bodyweight, in comparison to the cat whose skeleton makes up 13 per cent of its bodyweight. There are 46 bones that make up the spinal column, 7 cervical (the neck), 12 thoracic (the chest), 7 lumbar (the lower back), 4 sacral (the pelvis) and 16 coccigeal (the tail). The lumbar vertebrae are elongated to allow for considerable flexion and extension during hopping, but this makes them susceptible to fracture.

The characteristic hopping movement is made possible due to the fact that the hind legs are longer than the fore legs. Most of this elongation is below the stifle (the knee) in two bones, the tibia and fibula. The tibia is also particularly susceptible to fracture. Rabbits have 7 tarsal bones (the ankle) and 4 digits on both hind legs, and 9 carpal bones (the wrist) and 5 digits on both fore legs. Each digit has an associated toenail. If the rabbit is on a low-calcium diet and confined to a hutch with little opportunity to exercise, it may suffer from osteoporosis, making it particularly susceptible to limb and spinal fractures.

Rabbits have powerful hind legs and can kick violently, and if they struggle when they are picked up, or even if they stamp their feet violently on the ground, they may fracture one of their backbones (usually the seventh lumbar vertebra) and damage their spinal cord.

Anatomy and Physiology

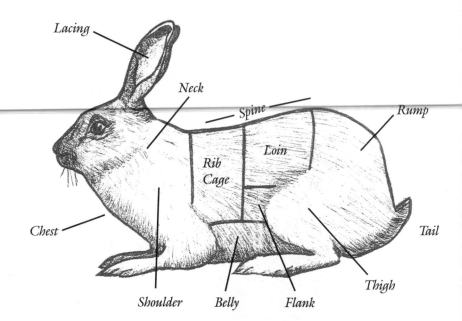

2. THE TEETH

Adult dentition		
Tooth type	Upper jaw	Lower jaw
Incisors	4	2
Canine	0	0
Premolars	6	4
Molars	6	6

Rabbits have 28 teeth, all of which grow continuously during their lifetime. They have two long upper and lower incisors, and an extra pair of tiny teeth behind the upper incisors known as peg teeth. These teeth act as 'doorstops' which prevent the lower incisors touching the upper gum. It is the presence of these peg teeth which sets rabbits and hares aside from other rodents in a sub-order known as Lagomorphs.

The incisors are designed for gnawing, and may grow up to 5 ins a year. If these teeth do not wear down properly they can overgrow and cause serious eating difficulties (see *Malocclusion*). There are 22 cheek teeth (premolars and molars), 6 on the top and 5 on the bottom on each side. These teeth are used for chewing, and the jaw is able to move forwards and backwards and from side to side. A wild rabbit may graze on grass for over four hours each day, chewing and wearing these teeth down.

Skeleton

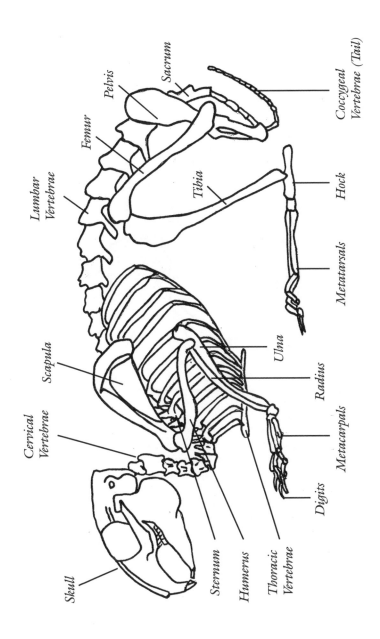

Sacrum

Pelvis

Femur

Coccygeal
Vertebrae (Tail)

Lumbar
Vertebrae

Tibia

Hock

Metatarsals

Scapula

Ulna

Cervical
Vertebrae

Radius

Skull

Metacarpals

Sternum

Humerus

Thoracic
Vertebrae

Digits

Skull

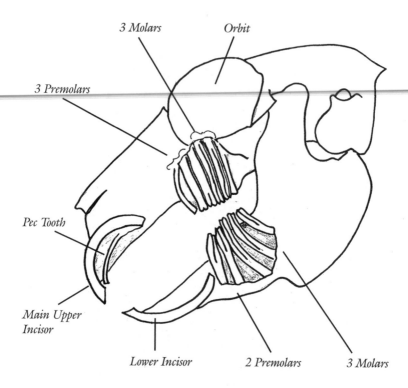

3 Molars

Orbit

3 Premolars

Pec Tooth

Main Upper Incisor

Lower Incisor

2 Premolars

3 Molars

The diet of the rabbit plays a very important role in keeping the teeth healthy. It is important that pet rabbits are given plenty of fibre in the form of hay, grass, wild plants and vegetables to encourage long periods of chewing which will promote good tooth wear. If rabbits only receive a bowl of dry food they may finish eating in 15-20 minutes, not long enough to wear the teeth properly. They also eat dry food with a crushing action rather than the desired side to side movement.

The amount of calcium in the diet is also important, as calcium is necessary for the formation of healthy teeth, and also healthy bones. If the diet is low in calcium the rabbit may suffer from osteomalacia of the jawbones (bone thinning) which will allow the teeth to move within their sockets and malocclusion can develop. The hay, greens and the dry food provide the calcium in the rabbit's diet. However, if the rabbit only selects its favourite pieces of the dry food, and leaves the rest, it is quite likely that it is receiving less calcium than it should be. Such selective feeding can be avoided by only feeding the rabbit a little of the dry food at one time, and not refilling the bowl until it is empty, or by feeding a ration of extruded nuggets or pellets, as each nugget is nutritionally balanced.

There is a gap between the incisors and the cheek teeth called the diastema. This gap is useful if it is necessary to dose the rabbit with medicine, or force-feed, as a dosing syringe can easily be placed in this space.

3. THE DIGESTIVE SYSTEM

The digestive system of the rabbit is huge and may account for between 10-20 per cent of its total bodyweight. If the intestines were laid out they would be more than 10 times the length of the rabbit. The rabbit's digestive system has evolved to survive on a very poor diet, and a special feature of the digestive process is known as caecotropy.

The rabbit manufactures soft faeces (called caecotrophs) which contain proteins and Vitamins B and K and which are covered in a protective mucous coat. These soft faeces are eaten by the rabbit, pass through the stomach acid and are digested and absorbed in the small intestine. This process of double digestion allows the rabbit to make the best use of the food it eats. These soft pellets are often mistaken for diarrhoea (see *Sticky Bottom Syndrome*).

The Digestive System

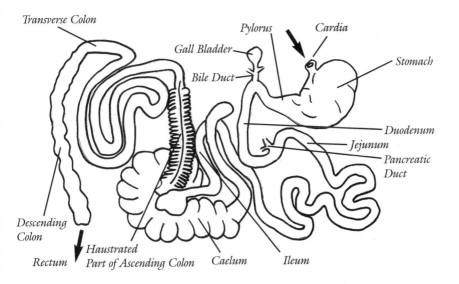

THE MOUTH

The rabbit is unable to see in front of its face, and cannot directly see the food it is eating. It relies on its senses of smell, and of touch. The upper lip of the rabbit is very sensitive and the rabbit will touch items to determine whether they are edible.

The mouth cavity is narrow, and the cheeks are pulled into the mouth. This makes examination of the back teeth very difficult in the conscious patient, and it is generally necessary to sedate the rabbit, so that special mouth gags and cheek dilators can be put in the mouth so that the teeth can be examined properly.

The tongue is large, and lies close to the bottom cheek teeth. If these teeth overgrow, even by a very small amount, their sharp edges can cause ulcers on the side of the tongue. Any rabbit that suddenly stops eating and starts dribbling (these ulcers are very painful), should be examined for teeth problems.

The rabbit has four pairs of salivary glands, called the parotid, submaxillary, sublingual and zygomatic. Of these the parotid is the largest; it extends from below the base of the ear to below the bottom jaw. The salivary glands produce two enzymes called amylase and galactosidase. These enzymes start to break down the food as it is chewed and to begin the process of digestion.

THE STOMACH
The rabbit, comparatively, has one of the largest stomachs of any mammal. It acts as a huge reservoir of food, and it should always be full. The arrangement of the entrance (cardia) and exit (pylorus) is such that the rabbit is unable to vomit. This special feature means that a rabbit need not, and should not, be starved before an anaesthetic.

The stomach juices are very acidic (pH 1-2) in the adult rabbit. This effectively sterilises the ingested food, and prevents any harmful bacteria moving further down the digestive system. However, if the rabbit eats a large amount of concentrated food that sits in the stomach as a huge ball, the centre of this ball may not be sterilised properly, and digestive upsets may follow. The stomach juices of the baby rabbit are not as acidic (usually pH 5-6) which means that young rabbits are far more susceptible to digestive disturbances and diarrhoea.

The acid and enzymes produced from the stomach wall begin to break down the food, particularly the proteins, and the food is then let out through the pylorus and moves into the small intestine.

THE SMALL INTESTINE
The small intestine is divided into three sections, the duodenum, the jejunum and the ileum. The function of the small intestine is to digest and absorb the nutrients from the diet. To aid the process of digestion the duodenum receives enzymes from the pancreas via the pancreatic duct, and bile acids from the gall bladder via the bile duct. The bile duct enters at the beginning of the duodenum, and the pancreatic duct enters at the end. The pancreatic enzymes break down the proteins, lipids (fats) and sugars and starches. The useful products of this digestion are absorbed through the wall of the jejunum into the bloodstream. The rest of the ingesta (mostly residual proteins and fibre) move through the ileocaecal valve into the large intestine.

THE LARGE INTESTINE
The large intestine is made up of the caecum and colon. The caecum is very large (about 10 times the volume of the stomach, and about 40 per cent of the total volume of the gastrointestinal tract). The colon separates the large and small fibre particles. The large particles of indigestible fibre are moved straight through the colon to form the hard droppings. The smaller fibre particles and other small incompletely digested food particles are moved backwards (by special muscles in

the wall of the colon called haustrae). This 'slurry' enters the caecum where it is broken down and fermented.

THE CAECUM

The caecum is the fermenting vat of the digestive system. To enable this fermentation to take place, it contains several species of 'helpful' bacteria (mostly *Bacteroides)*. The caecum also contains small amounts of potentially harmful bacteria (*Clostridia* and *E-coli*). In order that the balance of bacteria in the colon is such that the 'helpful' bacteria predominate, the diet must contain plenty of fibre and not too much protein and carbohydrate (i.e. not too much dry food and no sugary or starchy treats).

The end products of this fermentation are volatile fatty acids (VFAs) and caecotrophs. The VFAs are absorbed through the walls of the caecum and colon. The caecotrophs contain the fermented foodstuff, and are rich in Vitamins B and K, and high in protein. The caecal wall secretes a mucoid substance, which coats the caecotrophs before they are passed through the colon. These soft faeces are often referred to as 'night faeces' as they are usually produced at night. The arrival of these caecotrophs at the anus triggers a special nerve reflex, which makes the rabbit lick the anus and ingest these mucus-coated droppings as soon as they are passed (See *Caecotrophy*).

THE COLON

The colon absorbs fluids and sodium and chlorine from the ingesta as it passes through. It may also secrete potassium, to regulate the ion balance in the rabbit's system. What is left, after the absorption of the water, is passed via the anus as round hard droppings.

One of the most common malfunctions of the digestive system is when the rabbit produces large numbers of mucus-coated caecotrophs and does not eat them. Instead these faeces become stuck to the bottom, with a real risk of attracting flies (see *Fly Strike*).

This presentation is commonly mistaken for diarrhoea. There are several reasons why these caecal faeces accumulate. The rabbit may not be able to eat them (e.g. dental problems causing a sore mouth, obesity or large dewlap preventing the rabbit reaching the anus), or the diet may be unsuitable.

If the rabbit is fed too little fibre and an excess of protein and carbohydrate (the dry food), it will make more caecal pellets than it needs, and it may also feel satisfied from the absorption of proteins and carbohydrates and not feel the need to eat these droppings.

Another risk of feeding a low-fibre, high-concentrate diet is that the balance of 'helpful' and potentially harmful bacteria can alter. If the *Clostridia* get a chance to multiply they produce poisons called endotoxins which can cause rapid and fatal diarrhoea.

The whole digestive system should be in a constant state of movement. The muscles in the walls of the stomach, small and large intestine and caecum should be continuously working to move the ingested food through the digestive process. For the system to work efficiently, the rabbit needs a high-fibre diet. It is the indigestible coarse fibre (lignocellulose) which is most important.

If the system slows down or stops, there are potentially fatal consequences. If

63

there is food mixed with hair in the stomach this can dry out and act as a blockage (see *Hairball*). If the caecum stops moving, the harmful bacteria may multiply, releasing toxins (poisons) and causing diarrhoea.

The commonest reason why the guts slow down is due to a low-fibre diet; however, stress of any sort (through the release of the hormone adrenaline) can cause gut stasis. Any rabbit with gut stasis should receive urgent veterinary attention.

The rabbit has an unusual calcium metabolism. It absorbs all the digestible calcium from the diet, and the amount of calcium in the plasma (blood) is linked directly to the amount of calcium in the diet. The rabbit regulates the amount of calcium in the plasma by excreting any excess in the urine, rather than by other homeostatic mechanisms. If the rabbit is on a high-calcium diet, it will all be absorbed through the digestive system, and the resultant urine produced will be thick and creamy, even of toothpaste consistency (see *Sludgy Bladder*).

4. THE RESPIRATORY SYSTEM

Rabbits are obligate nose breathers, which means that they breathe through their noses. If a rabbit breathes through its mouth, it is in severe respiratory distress. The rabbit has a small chest cavity compared with the size and weight of its digestive system. It should never be held in such a way that the abdominal contents press on the chest, as the rabbit will find it difficult to breathe.

Rapid breathing may sometimes be a symptom of pain elsewhere in the body, and is seen in rabbits with bladder stones or womb cancer.

When the rabbit breathes, the air enters nostrils and moves through the nasal cavity. Here the air is warmed, and fine hairs called cilia trap any small dust particles and stop them from moving into the lungs. The air passes through the larynx (voice box) at the back of the mouth (the pharynx) and into the trachea (windpipe). The pharynx is shared between the respiratory and digestive system and it is here that a flap of skin called the epiglottis protects the top of the trachea. The epiglottis closes over the trachea when the rabbit swallows, to prevent food from getting into the lungs. The trachea enters the lungs and divides into two bronchi, which in turn divide into many smaller branches called bronchioles and these take the air to every part of the lungs. The bronchioles terminate in sacs called alveoli, and it is here that the oxygen is transferred to the bloodstream, and the waste product, carbon dioxide, is moved out.

The chest cavity is bordered by the ribs on either side, and is separated from the abdominal cavity by a powerful muscle called the diaphragm. The ribs and diaphragm move together like a pair of bellows to move air in and out of the chest. Like the dog, the left lung has two lobes, and the larger right lung has four lobes. The left and right lungs are totally separate and, if one side collapses, the other side can function normally.

Factors that damage the normal functioning of the respiratory system will make the rabbit more prone to respiratory infections. Ammonia associated with the build-up of urine in the hutch will weaken the lining of the nasal cavity. Other inhaled substances such as smoke, aerosol sprays etc. can also damage the nasal passages. If the environment is very dusty some inhaled particles may get past the cilia filter and reach the bronchi, where they may cause bronchitis.

The rabbit may carry bacteria called *Bordetella bronchiseptica* and, although this does not usually cause a respiratory infection in rabbits, it can be passed on to guinea pigs which will become ill. This risk should be considered if rabbits and guinea pigs are to be kept together. The rabbit may also carry bacteria called *Pasteurella* and these bacteria are responsible for both upper respiratory tract infection ('colds') and lower respiratory tract infection (pneumonia).

5. THE CARDIOVASCULAR SYSTEM

The rabbit has a relatively small heart which comprises around 0.3 per cent of its bodyweight. It is divided into two sides; the left side pumps the blood to the body, and the right side pumps the blood to the lungs. The left side is more muscular than the right as it needs to generate enough pressure to pump the blood around the body. Blood carrying carbon dioxide (waste product) enters the right side of the heart and is pumped into the lungs. Here the carbon dioxide is transferred to the lungs where it is expelled from the body as the rabbit breathes out. In return, oxygen is transferred to the bloodsteam from the lungs. The oxygenated blood passes to the left side of the heart where it is pumped to the body, leaving the heart through a large blood vessel called the aorta. Between each chamber of the heart there are special valves which ensure that the blood does not flow backwards between beats. The heart rate can vary from 180-250 beats per minute.

Rabbits can develop similar heart problems to those of man. Their arteries can become furred up, and if this happens to the arteries that supply the heart muscle, that area of muscle may die, affecting the function of the heart. Rabbits that are fed a high-calcium diet can develop calcification of the aorta. This results in a loss of elasticity of the blood vessel wall and leads, ultimately, to heart failure.

6. THE SENSE ORGANS

THE EYE

The rabbit is a prey animal, which means that in the wild it needs to have all-round vision so that it can see if it is about to be attacked. For this reason the eyes are sited towards the top of the head and each eye has a 190-degree field of vision. Rabbits are also very long-sighted. However, the position of the eyes means that the rabbit is not able to see directly in front of its nose, and if a hand approaches its face from directly in front, it may attack out of fear. For this reason rabbits should be approached from above so that they can see what is happening.

Each eye is like a minute camera. The eyeball itself is called the globe, and it sits in a bony cup called the orbit. Attached to the outside of the globe are a series of muscles that can move the globe around. The eye is filled with a fluid, which is being continually produced in the eye, and drained by the eye so that the amount of fluid in the eye is constant. If something goes wrong with this process the fluid can build up in the eye and the globe swells (glaucoma).

The coloured part of the eye is a muscle known as the iris. The iris has a central hole through which the light passes (the pupil). The iris can alter the size of the pupil so that the amount of light that enters the eye remains constant. In bright light the pupil becomes smaller as the iris contracts, and in dim light the iris relaxes and the pupil enlarges (dilates). Rabbits are able to dilate their pupils widely, and have a light sensitivity eight times that of man. The light passes from the pupil through the lens, which focuses the images. Muscles attached to the lens contract to make it change shape so that it can focus on different objects. The focused light is projected on to the retina, which is the lining at the back of the eye (equivalent to the photographic plate). In the retina light messages are transferred to nerve messages which take the translated images to the brain via the optic nerve.

The front surface of the eye is called the cornea. It is this surface that can be damaged by sharp objects such as straw stalks, causing a corneal ulcer. The surface of the cornea may then go cloudy, a process known as corneal oedema. Any damage to the eye should receive immediate veterinary attention.

The eye is surrounded by an upper and lower eyelid, and a third eyelid called the nictitating membrane. The third eyelid is well developed and moves right across the eye when the rabbit is asleep. Under the third eyelid is the Harderian gland which produces lubricating fluid. The Harderian gland is larger in males than in females and is largest during the breeding season. This gland may occasionally become enlarged and bulge out from under the third eyelid (a condition known as 'cherry eye'). A thin layer of skin that lies inside the eyelids and around the eye is known as the conjunctiva, and it is this area that becomes inflamed in conjunctivitis.

The eye is lubricated with tears, which are produced by the lachrymal glands and exit through the tear duct. Certain irritants such as cigarette smoke and dusty hay may cause the rabbit to produce excessive amounts of tears, and these may then run down the side of the face, making the fur matt together. The tears may also run down the face if the tear duct is blocked. The tear duct runs from a little hole in the conjunctiva under the third eyelid, over the tooth roots of the first upper premolar and incisors, and exits at the nares (nostrils). The route of the tear duct is not straight and it can easily become blocked or infected, particularly if there is impaction of the tooth roots into the tear duct.

THE EAR
The ears represent a large portion of the body surface in the average rabbit (approximately 12 per cent). However, with selective breeding there is a huge

A rabbit's ears are able to move independently.

diversity between the ears of a Netherland Dwarf and an English Lop. For wild rabbits hearing is their most important sense. Both ears are able to move independently, and the ears funnel sound waves into the ear, and even sounds of very low volume can be detected. In pet rabbits, however, this is only true for the prick-eared breeds; the lop-eared breeds do not have such good hearing. The ears of the rabbit are full of blood vessels, and are important in temperature regulation. Some of the blood vessels may be large and readily visible, and intravenous injections may be given here.

Normal earwax is golden and has no smell. Large accumulations of crusty wax may indicate an ear mite infection. Such a build-up of wax can lead to deafness, and deafness can cause a rabbit to exhibit fear aggression. Any rabbit that becomes uncharacteristically aggressive should have its ears examined.

7. THE URINARY SYSTEM

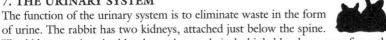

The function of the urinary system is to eliminate waste in the form of urine. The rabbit has two kidneys, attached just below the spine. The kidney receives its blood supply at relatively high blood pressure from the main artery from the heart (the aorta). The kidney works as a filtration system. It is made up of thousands of glomeruli, which are like little sieves; small particles such as urea (waste product) and glucose are sifted out, while larger molecules such as blood cells and protein stay in the bloodstream. The filtrate then passes through the tubules where some electrolytes (salts) may be returned to the bloodstream, and the urea then passes out of the kidney, and down a tube called the urether into the bladder. It is then voided from the bladder via the urethra as urine.

In kidney failure certain changes occur in the kidney. The nature of the glomeruli may change so that the sieve becomes more leaky, letting larger particles such as proteins escape into the urine. If this occurs over an extended period of time, the rabbit will lose more protein than it is taking in its diet and it will begin to lose weight.

If some of the glomeruli and their tubules die, the remaining filtration units may not be able to extract all the urea from the bloodstream and this urea will remain in the blood. Initially the rabbit makes some internal adjustments such as elongation of the remaining tubules, and finally the rabbit will drink more in an attempt to flush the urea from its bloodstream. However, because the initial internal adjustments work so well, the raised blood urea and increased thirst are only evident after two-thirds of the kidney are damaged, making the early stages of kidney failure impossible to detect.

Normal rabbit urine is clear to cloudy and may contain triple phosphate or calcium carbonate crystals. The rabbit has an unusual calcium metabolism, and if its diet is high in calcium there will be a lot of calcium passed out in the urine, and this can result in a 'sludgy urine' of almost toothpaste consistency. On some occasions the rabbit may produce urine which is dark red or orange in colour. This is quite normal, and related to the excretion of substances called porphyrins into the urine. These porphyrins may be released in times of stress. The urine can also be discoloured if the diet contains carrots or other sources of carotene, as these pigments are not completely broken down and are excreted in the urine.

8. THE REPRODUCTIVE SYSTEM

THE MALE
The male rabbit has two testicles which usually sit in pouches known as the scrotal sacs, between the hind legs. In the young rabbit the testicles are kept in the abdominal cavity, and at around 14 weeks of age they descend through the inguinal canals into the scrotal sacs. However, the inguinal canals remain open throughout life, and the rabbit is able to withdraw its testes into the abdomen in times of stress. On rare occasions the testicles may not descend, and remain in the abdominal cavity for its lifetime; this rabbit is known as a cryptorchid.

The testes produce spermatozoa which pass down tubules to a duct called the epididymus where they are stored. During mating the spermatozoa pass from the epididymus through a duct to the urethra where they are mixed with fluids from the prostate gland to produce the semen which is ejaculated from the erect penis.

The testes also produce the male hormone testosterone, which produces the male characteristics of the rabbit. It is for this reason that at sexual maturity (approximately five months of age) the behaviour of the male rabbit alters. The rabbit may begin to exhibit mounting behaviour (towards other rabbits or, if a house rabbit, towards other pets, legs, shoes etc.). The rabbit may also start spraying objects of its desire, and become aggressive. For pet rabbits neutering (castration) is recommended to eliminate these behaviour changes. Castration can be performed as soon as the testicles descend, and this will avoid these behaviour changes occurring in the first place. Castration removes both testicles surgically.

THE FEMALE
The female has two ovaries. Each ovary is linked via a fallopian tube to a separate uterine horn. The rabbit does not have a uterine body; instead, each uterine horn has its own entrance (the cervix) into the vagina. Does have 4-5 pairs of mammary glands and nipples; these are absent in the buck.

Rabbits do not have an oestrus cycle; instead they are induced ovulators, which means that they are in a constant state of sexual receptivity, and they ovulate when they are mated. Does reach sexual maturity around five months of age, although smaller breeds may mature earlier than larger breeds. Sexual maturity in the doe is also accompanied by behavioural changes. The doe may become aggressive, or she may mount-fight with a companion, even it is another doe. She may start spraying and circling like a buck. She may also begin digging or nesting.

If a doe is successfully mated, the gestation period is 30-33 days. Rabbits generally give birth in the early morning. Usually a few days before the birth the doe will start to pull fur from her dewlap, abdomen and sides to make a nest. The kits are born blind, hairless and helpless and usually remain in the nest for three weeks. Does only nurse their young for 3-5 minutes, usually early in the morning. The rest of the time they will remain away from their nest, so that they do not draw attention to their young. They are able to do this because their milk is so rich; one feed sustains the young for 24 hours. It is a common misconception when seeing the doe away from the nest that she must have abandoned her young, but this is not the case.

The Female Reproductive Tract

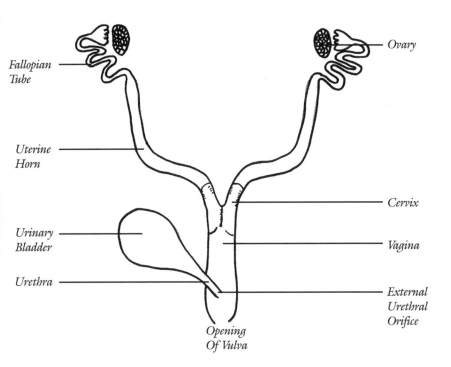

Fallopian Tube

Uterine Horn

Urinary Bladder

Urethra

Ovary

Cervix

Vagina

External Urethral Orifice

Opening Of Vulva

If the mating is unsuccessful the doe may spontaneously ovulate and this will result in a false pregnancy (pseudopregnancy). A doe mounting another doe can also trigger ovulation. Some does that live alone may be able to self-induce ovulation and exhibit recurrent false pregnancies. False pregnancy usually lasts 18 days, during which time the does may become increasingly aggressive, and exhibit fur-pulling and nest building.

If the doe is a pet, it is recommended that she be neutered at six months of age. This removes the negative behavioural characteristics associated with sexual maturity and subsequent false pregnancies. It is also an important preventative measure, as 80 per cent of entire (un-neutered) does will suffer from womb cancer by the time they are six years old. Neutering (spaying) involves the surgical removal of both ovaries, uterine horns and cervices under general anaesthetic.

9. THE SKIN AND SCENT MARKING GLANDS
The female has a large flap of skin under the chin called the dewlap. It is from here that the female pulls most of the hair when she builds a nest. In some cases the dewlap can become so large that the rabbit may not be able to practise normal caecotrophy (coprophagy). It is possible surgically to reduce the dewlap in these cases. Castrated males may also develop dewlaps.

Rabbits do not have footpads; instead they have a covering of fur over the toes and metatarsals. When a rabbit sits down, the whole of the lower legs from the hock (ankles) downwards touch the ground. Overweight rabbits, or those with little fur covering, may develop ulcerated pressure sores on their hocks. This can occur if the surface of the hutch, or bedding, is rough. House rabbits can develop carpet burn in this area too. The rabbit has sweat glands that open on its feet.

Rabbits are strongly territorial and have three sets of glands used for scent marking behaviour. They have specialised submandibular glands which open on the underside of the chin, and the rabbit rubs its chin on items of its territory, particularly new or novel items (known as 'chinning'). It has a pair of anal glands, and a pair of inguinal glands which are sited in deep pockets either side of the genitals. The inguinal glands produce a white odorous discharge; this is normal.

The activity of the scent glands is hormone-dependent and related to the level of sexual activity. Neutered rabbits do less scent marking; however, they will still 'chin' new objects in their environment.

CHAPTER 9

A-Z OF RABBIT DISEASES

1. **Alphabetical listing of rabbit diseases**

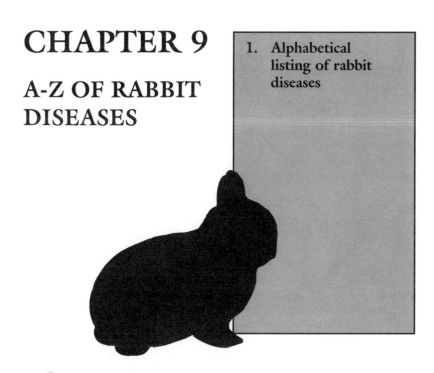

ABSCESS

A swelling on the body containing pus.

Signs: Abscesses can appear anywhere on the body, commonly around the face. They are generally soft swellings, although they may become hard and warm as the pus builds up. Despite their size they are usually not painful and the rabbit may remain well.

Cause: Abscesses are caused by a bacterial infection. This may be the result of a bite from another rabbit, or, in the case of abscesses around the face, be associated with a tooth root infection. Tooth root abscesses may also involve infection within the jawbone (osteomyelitis) and in these cases a bony lump may be felt under the chin.

Treatment: If possible the abscess can be removed surgically. Alternatively, the abscess can be lanced and drained, and treated with antibiotics. Unfortunately in many cases it is not possible to cure the abscess; however, it may be controlled with long-term antibiotics and repeated draining.

AGGRESSION

Aggression is perceived as a behaviour problem where the rabbit reacts to a situation by grunting, pouncing and biting. The aggression can be directed towards other rabbits, or its owner.

Signs: The rabbit may pounce towards another rabbit or its owner, while grunting and growling. It can inflict a painful nip, and wounds caused by two rabbits fighting can be quite severe.

Cause: A rabbit may be aggressive through fear. Rabbits cannot see well in front of their noses and, if their owner's hand approaches them from in front, they may attack it as they cannot see it properly. For this reason, rabbits are best approached with a hand from above the body.

Rabbits can also exhibit food aggression and territory aggression. Sexual maturity will lead to many behavioural changes including aggression associated with false pregnancy in the doe. At sexual maturity, rabbits of the same sex that have been paired together may begin fighting. Pain of any kind may cause a rabbit to become short-tempered and aggressive.

Treatment: Aggression of either sex associated with sexual maturity will improve after neutering. However, two bucks may still not live together harmoniously even if they are both neutered.

The cause of fear aggression must be investigated; when approaching a rabbit, the hand should come from above the body, and should be clean. Rabbits are particularly fearful of odours such as engine oil, strong perfumes, and predators (dogs and cats) unless they have become accustomed to them.

Food aggression stems from the natural instinct to guard precious food sources, as they are generally scarce in the wild. It may help to provide several food sources or scatter the food over the floor. Rabbits that are able to spend hours grazing on hay and fibrous plants are likely to be more satisfied than those that receive just a single bowl of pellets.

ALLERGIES

Allergies occur when the body reacts in an exaggerated manner to an allergen. An allergen can be a protein or non-protein substance, which causes an allergy. This condition may also be referred to as atopy.

Signs: The commonest symptom is a clear discharge from both eyes, and the rabbit may sneeze occasionally. The rabbit remains well in itself. More severe cases may show skin crusting and soreness around the ears and nose and even inside the legs and on the abdomen.

Cause: Dusty hay or bedding are common causes. House rabbits may be exposed to other potential allergens such as cigarette smoke, furniture polish and other household aerosols.

Treatment: Where possible, the allergen should be identified and removed from the environment. The eyes can be bathed with a dilute saline solution and, if necessary, eye drops can be used. The more severely affected cases will need steroid medication prescribed by a veterinary surgeon.

ALOPECIA
Loss of hair from the body.
Signs: Hair loss may occur from any part of the body, and may be accompanied by pruritis (itching).
Cause: Hair loss associated with intense dandruff is caused by a mite *(See Cheyletiella)*. This condition is pruritic. Does will pluck hair from their dewlap and abdomen prior to giving birth, or during a false pregnancy. Rabbits that form a close pair-bond may overgroom each other to such an extent that they cause areas of alopecia, particularly around the ears. More severe overgrooming can lead to extensive fur loss *(See Barbering)*.
Treatment: Cheyletiella is treated by antiparasitic injections or shampoos. The coat can be combed with a fine flea-comb to remove the dandruff. Does that have false pregnancies should be spayed.

AMPUTATION
The loss of a limb may be necessary if the rabbit has a complicated or severely infected fracture that is irreparable. Cancer of a limb bone is rare, but is another indication for amputation. Rabbits cope extremely well with the loss of a limb. They may experience some problems of urinary soiling, but this can be minimised by providing soft absorbent bedding.

ANOREXIA
A loss of appetite.
Signs: The rabbit refuses all food, or becomes selective about what it eats.
Cause: There are many causes of anorexia. In all cases immediate veterinary attention must be sought because, if the rabbit stops eating for more than two days, it may develop liver failure. Overgrown back teeth are a very common reason why the rabbit stops eating. The sharp edges of the back (molar) teeth may grow toward the tongue or cheek causing painful ulcers. If the back teeth are overgrown the rabbit is likely to dribble and the insides of its forelegs may become damp and matted where it wipes its face with its paws.

Gastric stasis and bloat are frequent causes of anorexia. The rabbit will look dull, be reluctant to move and may have a swollen abdomen. If the gastrointestinal system stops moving, the ingested food, and any hair, can cause a blockage *(See Hairball)*.

Pain of any sort will quickly stop a rabbit from eating, and any rabbit that stops eating for no apparent reason should receive some pain relief. Stress can also lead to anorexia.
Treatment: The cause of the anorexia should be investigated and treated accordingly. Whatever the cause, it is important to provide the rabbit with fluids and calories (force-fed if necessary) in order to prevent liver failure. Fluids can be given by mouth via a syringe or dropper, or may need to be given by the veterinary surgeon intravenously or under the skin. Pain relief can also be given by the veterinary surgeon. The rabbit can be tempted with leafy greens such as dandelions, parsley and carrot tops, or, if necessary, a blend of pineapple juice, soaked rabbit pellets and pureed vegetable baby food in a 1:1:1 ratio can be fed

little and often by syringe. Puréed bananas are another favourite. Probiotics are also helpful; these are usually a powder that contains a mixture of live bacteria and electrolytes.

ANTIBIOTIC-INDUCED DIARRHOEA
The rabbit's normal digestive system contains a balance of beneficial and harmful bacteria. Certain antibiotics may destroy the beneficial bacteria and allow the harmful ones to multiply, produce toxins (poisons) and cause enterotoxaemia.

Signs: The rabbit becomes depressed and anorexic following antibiotic administration. The diarrhoea is watery brown and may contain blood and mucus. Death occurs in 24-48 hours. Some rabbits may bloat and die before developing diarrhoea.

Cause: Certain antibiotics, such as cephaloridine, cephalexin and penicillin, which have a narrow spectrum of activity selectively destroy the beneficial bacteria and let the harmful *Clostridium spiriformes* proliferate.

Treatment: Prevention is better than cure in this case. Veterinary surgeons will always use the safer broad-spectrum antibiotics, such as enrofloxacin (Baytril) unless the condition specifically requires an alternative. An example where penicillin is specifically indicated is in the treatment of rabbit syphilis (Vent Disease). The rabbit should be given a probiotic (a cocktail of live beneficial bacteria) while it is on antibiotics. As long as the rabbit is on a healthy diet of hay and green food the effect of any antibiotic on its digestive system should be minimal. If one of the more narrow-spectrum antibiotics is used, it is better to give it by injection than to give it orally.

ARTHRITIS
This is defined as inflammation of the joint.

Signs: Reduced mobility. Instead of hopping, the rabbit may move both back legs together, or shuffle. Because of the limited movement the rabbit is more prone to urinary and faecal soiling.

Cause: The most common cause is age-associated 'wear and tear'. This is also known as degenerative joint disease.

Treatment: Pain relief can be given. The bedding should be made as soft as possible, and, for rabbits prone to urinary soiling, absorbent bedding such as Vetbed can be used. If the rabbit is litter-trained it should have a tray with a low rim, e.g. a baking tray, that it can access easily.

AUTO IMMUNE DISEASE
This is a rare disease produced by the rabbit as it responds to the presence of its own cells with an excessive immune reaction.

Signs: Lesions around the face, nose, lips and chin that blister and then scab over.

Cause: The rabbit inappropriately produces antibodies that attack the cells in the skin around the face. This is a rare condition; other conditions that may present like this are rabbit syphilis, and allergy (atopy).

Treatment: High doses of steroids can be prescribed by a veterinary surgeon.

B

BARBERING

Barbering is the term used when a rabbit chews its own coat, or the coat of another rabbit.

Signs: If the rabbit is chewing itself there will be patches of hair loss and sore skin over its body. If a rabbit is being barbered, the hair loss may be around the head and neck. Rabbits that chew hair are more prone to developing hairballs if their gastrointestinal system moves slowly.

Cause: The irritation caused by parasitic infection *(see Cheyletiella, Fleas)* will cause a rabbit to chew its coat. However, most cases of barbering are associated with boredom, and a low-fibre diet. Occasionally it may be the most dominant rabbit in a group that barbers its companions and, in this instance it may be necessary to keep it separate.

Treatment: Parasitic skin disease must be investigated and treated accordingly.

A high-fibre diet, i.e. plentiful hay, edible wild plants and greens should be provided. In its natural state the rabbit would forage and graze for at least 4-6 hours daily; it is no wonder that pet rabbits become easily bored with a bowl of dry food which takes them a fraction of this time to consume. Scattering some of the food around the rabbit's environment so that it has to search for it can also prevent boredom. Toys can also be provided, cat toys are suitable, or the rabbit can be provided with cardboard tubes, plastic flower pots etc. which will provide hours of amusement. Edible toys such as straw coasters and baskets are also suitable.

A single rabbit that is barbering itself will benefit from neutering, and pairing with a companion rabbit.

BLADDER STONES

(See Urinary Calculi)

BLOAT

Bloat is seen when the stomach fills up with gas. The caecum can also become gas filled *(See Caecal Tympany)*.

Signs: Symptoms can appear suddenly. The rabbit will be reluctant to move, and the abdomen will feel swollen and hard. The rabbit may grind its teeth in pain. Often no droppings are passed.

Cause: The rabbit's gastrointestinal system is designed to be moving all the time and, for it to function properly, it needs plenty of coarse fibre in the diet. If the guts stop moving, the ingested food contents may start to ferment and create gas that fills the stomach and intestines. As the rabbit stops eating it draws fluid from the ingested food causing any food and hair to become dry and impacted leading, in some cases, to a secondary blockage. Diets that are low in fibre and high in protein and carbohydrates (e.g. dry food and treats, with little or no hay and green foods) make this condition most likely. Stress of any sort causes the body to release a hormone called adrenaline that also slows the gastrointestinal system down.

Treatment: Bloat is a genuine emergency, and the rabbit should be taken to a veterinary surgeon immediately. The treatment will involve drugs to try and get the gastrointestinal system moving again, and pain relief. The rabbit will also need plenty of fluids, either intravenously, subcutaneously (under the skin) or orally via a dropper or syringe.

When the gas is building up, harmful bacterial have a chance to multiply and produce toxins (causing enterotoxaemia) so an antibiotic and a probiotic may be given.

The rabbit may also need to be force-fed with a mixture of pineapple juice, soaked rabbit pellets and pureed baby food in a 1:1:1 mixture, until it starts eating on its own. Gentle exercise should be encouraged to help the gas move. It may take 3-4 days of intensive nursing before the rabbit improves, and some cases are, unfortunately, fatal.

BLUE FUR
A moist dermatitis associated with a *Pseudomonas* infection of the skin which causes the skin to take on a blue-green colouration.
Signs: Blue-green discolouration of any area of fur that stays permanently moist.
Cause: The infection is caused by the bacterium *Pseudomonas aeruginosa*. It affects any area that stays moist with saliva, urine or water from permanently leaking water bottles. Some rabbits chin their water bottle and it is commonly the dewlap that becomes affected.
Treatment: The area should be kept dry, and treated with antibiotics. Water bottles are thought to harbour the bacterium and should be cleaned regularly.

CAECAL TYMPANY
The caecum (the large fermenting vat in the digestive system) fills up with gas.
Signs: The rabbit is depressed and has a swollen abdomen. If the rabbit is picked up, its abdomen may sound like a half-full hot water bottle, as the fluid gut contents splash around in the caecum. The caecum contains a balance of beneficial and pathogenic bacteria and, if its function is impaired, the harmful bacteria can multiply and produce toxins, which can be fatal.
Cause: A low-fibre diet will cause the slow passage of food through the intestines, and a build-up of food in the caecum. If there are excesses of starches and sugars in the diet (e.g. too much dry food, too many sweet treats and bread), then this provides 'fuel' allowing the harmful bacteria to multiply.
Treatment: As for bloat, treatment is directed at encouraging the movement of the guts and preventing the multiplication of harmful bacteria with an antibiotic, and a probiotic.

CAECOTROPHY

This is the perfectly normal behaviour of eating the soft faeces (caecotrophs) that are passed at night direct from the anus. The rabbit's digestive system is designed to function on a minimal diet, and these soft faeces contain proteins and vitamins which are absorbed on their second passage through the intestines. If the rabbit is on a high-carbohydrate, low-fibre diet, it may produce excessive amounts of these faeces which become stuck to its fur *(See Sticky Bottom Syndrome)*. Caecotrophy may also be impaired if the rabbit has a physical problem such as arthritis, obesity, or mouth ulcers associated with overgrown back teeth *(See Malocclusion)*.

CANDIDIASIS

A yeast infection of the skin more commonly known as Thrush.
Signs: A moist dermatitis, especially under the chin and dewlap.
Cause: The infection is caused by the yeast *Candida albicans*. The yeast thrives in damp conditions, and is more likely to occur if the rabbit's face stays wet from a leaky water bottle, or if the rabbit dribbles excessively.
Treatment: The area should be bathed daily with a chlorhexidine solution, and daily application of an anti-mycotic should clear the condition in 10-14 days. The face should be kept dry and, if the rabbit is dribbling, its teeth may need attention *(see Malocclusion)*.

CASTRATION

Castration is the surgical removal of both testicles. As the testes produce the male hormone testosterone, this procedure removes the undesirable male characteristics associated with sexual maturity.

Castration eliminates such behaviours as mounting, spraying and aggression. A castrated male can form a close pair-bond with a doe (preferably also neutered). Castrated males are easier to house-train and their urine has less smell (important for house rabbits). Neutering also prevents unwanted breeding.

In general, two bucks will not live together without fighting. The exception may be two brothers that have been together since birth, and neutered before they reach sexual maturity.

CATARACT

An opacity of the lens in the eye.
Signs: The centre of the eye becomes progressively white and cloudy. A complete cataract can lead to blindness of the affected eye.
Cause: Some cataracts are congenital, others occur as part of the ageing process.
Treatment: No treatment is required, as the pet rabbit can cope adequately with reduced eyesight.

CELLULITIS

This condition is associated with a bacterial infection. An area of skin, usually around the neck, becomes hot, swollen and painful.
Signs: The rabbit develops a painful, swollen area, usually around the neck. The

rabbit is feverish, with a temperature of 104-108 degrees F. The lesion may develop into an abscess, or the skin may turn blackened (necrotic) and die.

Cause: The condition is caused by the same bacteria that are associated with abscess development, *Staphylococcus aureus* and *Pasteurella multocida*.

Treatment: The rabbit should be given antibiotics and pain relief. Cool baths will also help bring the temperature down.

CHEYLETIELLA
This mite causes a parasitic disease of the skin known as Cheyletiellosis. It is the commonest skin disease in rabbits.

Signs: Patches of hair loss, especially on the neck and back, which are accompanied by intense scurf. The condition is mildly pruritic (itchy). It is possible for owners to catch this mite; in people it causes a short-lived itchy rash.

Cause: A mite called *Cheyletiella parasitovorax* causes this condition. The mite does not burrow but lives off the surface of the skin, biting the surface and feeding on the serum below.

Treatment: Ivermectin, an antiparasitic treatment, is highly effective, and can be given as a course of injections, or as drops on the skin. Shampooing will reduce the scurf. As rabbit hair is so fine it is better to use a hair dryer than a towel to dry it. The hutch should also be well cleaned and can be sprayed with an environmental flea control product.

COCCIDIOSIS
Coccidia are the commonest parasite of the rabbit. They are tiny protozoal parasites that are found in the intestines, liver and bile ducts. Not all species of Coccidia (there are twelve different types) cause disease, and healthy rabbits can carry Coccidia without showing any symptoms. The adult parasites live in the lining of the intestines or liver. The eggs (oocytes) are passed out in the droppings. The oocysts thrive in damp environments. If the oocysts are then eaten by the rabbit they move into the intestinal wall, develop into adults and the life cycle is completed.

Signs: Symptoms of hepatic Coccidiosis (caused by those that colonise the liver) are a general unthriftiness, or signs of liver failure, jaundice, diarrhoea, a swollen abdomen and death. Signs of intestinal Coccidiosis (caused by those that colonise the intestines) are most apparent in young rabbits and include diarrhoea (often containing blood and mucus), weight loss, anorexia and, in severe cases, dehydration and death.

Cause: Twelve species of Coccidia parasitize the rabbit, though not all cause disease. Hepatic Coccidiosis is caused by *Eimeria stiedae,* Intestinal Coccidiosis is often caused by mixed infections of *Eimeria magna, perforans* and *media*.

Treatment: Antibiotics can be given in the drinking water. Some rabbit pellets contain a coccidiostat (a drug which controls coccidia), and this may be fed to rabbits all the time. Attention to the environment is most important as the oocysts thrive in damp conditions and can live for several months outside the rabbit. Hutches should be cleaned regularly, and deep litter systems avoided. If the rabbit is in a pen outside, the location of the run should be changed regularly.

CONJUNCTIVITIS

Inflammation of the conjunctiva.

Signs: The conjunctiva of one or both eyes is reddened and sore. There may be a clear or white discharge from the affected eye.

Cause: Conjunctivitis can be an allergic response to an irritant such as dusty hay or cigarette smoke. If the rabbit is on a high-protein diet it will produce a lot of ammonia in its urine and this can irritate the eyes. Tear duct infections are usually accompanied by conjunctivitis.

Treatment: The source of the irritant should be removed. If infection is present, antibiotic and anti-inflammatory eye drops should be used.

COPROPHAGY

(See Caecotrophy)

CORNEAL ULCERATION

If the surface of the cornea is damaged an ulcer develops. This is an area of weakness in the cornea until healing is complete.

Signs: The rabbit will hold its eye half-closed or shut with discomfort. On close inspection of the eye, the ulcer will be visible as a little pit on the surface. The area of the cornea around the ulcer may be cloudy as the fluid movement in and out of the cornea is disturbed (corneal oedema). As the ulcer heals, minute blood vessels can be seen creeping from the edge of the eye towards the ulcer (corneal vascularisation). If the ulcer is very deep, and the corneal surface very thin, the fluid in the eye may push the surface outwards, so that it looks like a bubble on the eye. The worst outcome of this is that the bubble may burst and the fluid from the eye can leak out.

Cause: The most common cause of an ulcer is a poke from a sharp piece of bedding. Straw causes the most eye injuries. Corneal ulceration can occur following conjunctivitis, entropion or a tear duct infection.

Treatment: If there is a discharge, the eye should be bathed with warm water. Eye cream or drops containing antibiotics are necessary while the ulcer is healing. Complete healing can take several weeks. If the damage to the eye is so severe that healing is impossible, the eye can be removed surgically.

CRYPTORCHIDISM

One or more testicles may be absent from the scrotum. The testicles of the male rabbit do not descend from the abdominal cavity until the rabbit is 12-14 weeks of age. The channel through which they descend is called the inguinal canal. This canal remains open throughout the rabbit's life, and in times of stress the rabbit is able to withdraw the testicles back into the abdomen. A cryptorchid male is a rabbit who has one or both testicles that never descend into the scrotum.

CYSTIC MASTITIS

A condition of the older female rabbit. One or more mammary glands may become cystic and swollen and discharge clear fluid from the nipple.

Signs: One or more mammary glands become swollen, and have a clear discharge. The doe remains well in herself.

Cause: This is not an infectious form of mastitis. Instead it is associated with uterine adenocarcinoma and endometrial hyperplasia, which are both womb changes seen in the older doe.

Treatment: Ovariohysterectomy. The affected gland can be removed at the same time, but this is not always necessary as the cysts may regress 3-4 weeks after surgery.

CYSTITIS
An inflammation of the lining of the bladder.

Signs: Blood in the urine (Haematuria), and pain on urination. The rabbit may make frequent attempts to urinate. House rabbits may show a sudden loss of house-training habits. The hind legs and perineal area may become urine-soiled.

Cause: Cystitis is a bacterial infection, usually caused by *E-coli* or *Pseudomonas*. Rabbit urine normally contains triple phosphate and calcium carbonate crystals, but if these build up they can irritate the bladder lining and predispose to cystitis.

Treatment: The bladder may be X-rayed to rule out the presence of bladder stones. If cystitis is diagnosed, the rabbit will need a long course of antibiotics. The urine can be tested for the presence of bacteria and the antibiotic chosen on the results of this test. It may help to acidify the urine by adding ascorbic acid (Vitamin C) to the drinking water. A change of diet can help reduce the number of crystals in the urine *(See Sludgy Bladder)*.

D

DEMODECTIC MANGE
This is a rare skin condition in rabbits caused by a burrowing mite. It is only seen in rabbits that are immunocompromised.

Signs: A moist dermatitis, with small pustules 2-4 mm in diameter. It is not pruritic (itchy).

Cause: Demodecosis is caused by the mite *Demodex cuniculi*. The mite burrows into the hair follicles and can only be identified by examining skin scrapes under the microscope. The mite is probably present in small numbers in most rabbits and kept under control by their immune system. However, if the immune system is not functioning properly the mite is able to multiply and cause infection.

Treatment: Treatment usually involves weekly injections of ivermectin, but a wash containing amitraz can also be used.

DEWLAP
The dewlap is a large fold of skin under the chin, most prominent in does. This is where the doe pulls her fur from to make a nest. However, if it becomes especially large it can become a site for bacterial infections, and it

can also hinder the normal practice of coprophagy. **In these instances it is possible to reduce it surgically, but generally its presence is no cause for concern. Occasionally, it is a site of abscess development** *(See Abscess)*.

DIABETES

A condition where the blood sugar (glucose) is raised above the normal level and excess sugar is excreted in the urine. It is thought to be extremely rare in the rabbit.

Signs: The rabbit is thirsty and passes excessive amounts of urine. The appetite is generally good, but the rabbit loses weight. These symptoms are more commonly associated with kidney failure. Glucose may be present in the urine (dipstick test), and the blood glucose is raised. However, stress and liver disorders can cause an increase in blood and urine glucose, so these results are interpreted with care.

Cause: Diabetes is caused if the pancreas fails to produce insulin. Insulin is a hormone that transports glucose from the bloodstream into the body tissues where it is used as energy. If the glucose stays in the bloodstream it is excreted in the urine. The glucose pulls water with it as it passes through the kidneys, and the rabbit drinks more to compensate for this water loss.

Treatment: If diabetes is suspected the rabbit's diet should be altered to one of high fibre, and reduced carbohydrate. This means feeding plenty of hay, greens and wild plants, and restricting the dry food. Any sugary treats should be replaced with fruit and vegetable ones.

DIARRHOEA

True diarrhoea (enteritis) exists when all the motions are loose and watery. Rabbits that produce hard droppings and soft mucous droppings simultaneously do not have diarrhoea *(See Sticky Bottom Syndrome)*.

Signs: Profuse watery motions, often lethargy, anorexia and a staring hair coat. Dehydration and death may follow within 24-48 hours.

Cause: Diarrhoea can be caused by bacteria, viruses, protozoa, a dietary change, following antibiotic use, and in times of stress. Rabbits of 1-14 days of age are usually affected by *E-coli*, rabbits of 4-8 weeks of age are susceptible to weaning enteritis associated with *Clostridia* infection, older rabbits can be affected by *E-coli*, *Clostridium piliforme* (Tyzzer's Disease), and *Salmonella*. Rabbits of 7-14 weeks of age are at risk from Mucoid Enteritis. Diarrhoea associated with a dietary change can occur if the rabbit is fed an excess of a vegetable it is not used to. Green food should make up a large proportion of the diet, but any unfamiliar item should be introduced slowly. Wild plants do not generally cause diarrhoea, with the exception of dandelions which are laxative in action.

Treatment: Whatever the cause, the treatment protocol is similar. The rabbit should be kept in warm, clean surroundings. Fluid replacement is very important. Fluids can be given orally at a rate of 50-100ml/kg bodyweight/day. A probiotic (a substance containing live 'helpful' gut bacteria) will help keep the balance of gastrointestinal bacteria normal. Antibiotics may be given.

The rabbit should be tempted with good-quality hay and astringent wild plants (e.g. shepherd's purse, blackberry and raspberry leaves). These plants are binding and a natural way to stop diarrhoea. A preparation containing kaolin can be given orally to help bind up the liquid faeces. *(See also Mucoid Enteritis, Viral Haemorrhagic Disease and Coccidiosis)*.

DRIBBLING
Excessive salivation is usually associated with mouth disorders. The fur under the chin can become sore and infected if it remains permanently damp.
Signs: The rabbit is permanently wet around its lips and chin. Often the insides of the fore legs are wet and matted as the rabbit wipes its mouth with its paws. If the salivation is associated with tooth disorders the rabbit may stop eating.
Cause: The most common cause is dental disorders. The front teeth (incisors) can overgrow, as can the back teeth *(See Malocclusion)*. The back teeth can grow so that sharp edges of the teeth grow into the tongue or cheek causing painful mouth ulcers.
Treatment: The underlying dental disorders must be treated. If the back teeth are growing abnormally, they can be clipped and filed under sedation. However, as these teeth grow all the time, the problem is likely to recur, and some rabbits require dental treatment every 6-8 weeks. A good diet with plenty of hay, grass and greens will help encourage the side-to-side chewing action which promotes better wear of these back teeth. The skin under the chin should be bathed, and any infection treated *(See Candidiasis and 'Blue Fur')*.

DYSTOCIA
This defines a difficulty in parturition (the birth process).
Signs: The female rabbit prepares a nest 30-33 days after mating, but produces no young. She may have a bloody discharge from the vulva. Birth usually occurs in the early hours of the morning and is, therefore, not usually seen, but if the doe is watched in labour she will be seen straining unproductively. After a while she will become tired and stop straining, and the bloody discharge will be the only sign that labour started.
Cause: Birth is difficult if the foetus is oversized, or if it is wrongly positioned in the birth canal.
Treatment: It may be possible to restart parturition with a hormone injection. However, if the foetus is stuck, the doe will need a Caesarean section. The young produced as a result of the surgery are unlikely to survive, but a Caesarean should save the doe, if it is done before she has become too exhausted.

E

EAR MITES
Ear mites live in the ear of the rabbit, causing irritation, and a build-up of crusty earwax.

Signs: Early cases may just have mildly pruritic (itchy) ears. More advanced cases will have thick, yellow-grey crusts in the ear canal, and the ears will be red, inflamed and very itchy. Rarely the rabbit may develop sores and crusts on the face and legs.

Cause: Ear mite infestation is caused by the mite *Psoroptes cuniculi*. The mites may reach 0.7mm in size and can be visible to the naked eye.

Treatment: The rabbit can be given a course of ivermectin injections. If the earwax is to be removed the rabbit should be sedated, as it can be very painful. Cleaning the ears may not be necessary as, once treatment is underway, the crusts will dry up and fall out. In-contact rabbits should also be treated, and the environment should be sprayed with an environmental flea spray as the female mites can survive several weeks away from the host, and cause re-infestation.

ENDOMETRIAL HYPERPLASIA

The endometrium is the lining of the womb. As the rabbit ages, the endometrium becomes thickened and cystic. It may then become cancerous.

Signs: The doe will pass blood intermittently at the end of urination. Blood clots may appear in the urine. The mammary glands may also become cystic, and occasionally discharge clear fluid.

Cause: These changes are characteristic of the womb as the rabbit ages, presumably because it is in a state of perpetual hormone overload from sexual maturity onwards.

Treatment: Neutering (ovariohysterectomy) is curative. Once the ovaries and womb are removed, the cystic mammary glands will generally regress.

ENDOMETRIAL VENOUS ANEURYSM

A condition of the uterus where both uterine horns fill up with blood.

Signs: The female rabbit passes blood either during or at the end of urination. Initially it may occur independently; in the later stages of the condition large amounts of blood may be passed.

Cause: Both uterine horns fill up with blood. The reason why this can sometimes happen is unknown.

Treatment: Other causes of blood in the urine must be eliminated *(See Haematuria)*. Ovariohysterectomy will cure the condition.

ENTROPION

The upper or lower eyelids turn inwards allowing the eyelashes to rub on the eye causing corneal ulceration.

Signs: The rabbit will keep its eye half-closed with discomfort. On close examination the affected part of the eyelid is seen turning inwards, causing a corneal ulcer where the eyelashes are constantly rubbing the eye.

Cause: This is usually a congenital deformity. It can also occur in aged rabbits if their eyes sink back into their sockets allowing the eyelids to turn in.

Treatment: The deformity can be corrected surgically. Any corneal ulceration can be treated with eye cream or drops containing antibiotic.

EYE

A clear discharge from the eye occurs if excessive tears are produced. This can occur as a result of an allergy *(See Allergies)*. The tear duct runs over the roots of the upper premolar and incisor roots, and these can irritate and block the duct, causing tears to run down the face. A thick white discharge is associated with dacrocystitis *(See Tear Duct Infection)*. The conjunctiva can become inflamed *(See Conjunctivitis)*. The surface of the eye can become damaged *(See Corneal Ulceration)*. Fatty white deposits on the surface of the eye (corneal lipidosis) are normal, as is the development of grey cloudy areas on the centre of the eye (corneal dystrophy). The lens in the centre of the eye can become cloudy *(See Cataract)*.

Certain conditions can make the eye look swollen. Glaucoma, the increase in fluid in the eye, is rare; more common is the development of an abscess behind the eye following a tear duct infection, or associated with a tooth root infection *(See Retrobulbar Abscess)*.

F

FALSE PREGNANCY
(See Pseudopregnancy)

FLEAS

Fleas are a group of ectoparasites that can live away from the animal but, in order to breed, they need a host to feed from. Fleas are a major vector of the mxyomatosis virus.

Signs: Fleas can be seen moving in the coat as brown wingless insects 1-2 mm long. Small black flea droppings (digested blood) may also be found. They may cause irritation and itching.

Cause: Outdoor rabbits may harbour the rabbit flea (*Spilopysyllus cuniculi*) and the stickfast flea (*Echidophagis mymecobil*). House rabbits are most likely to come into contact with the cat and dog flea (*Ctenocephalides felis* and *canis*).

Treatment: The rabbit can be sprayed with a flea spray containing pyrethrin. Other sprays are not suitable. There are various herbal preparations available which claim to be effective against fleas. An environmental flea spray can be used around the hutch or house to kill any eggs, larvae and adults that are living off the host. It is very important to vaccinate the rabbit against mxyomatosis.

FLOPPY RABBIT SYNDROME
(See Potassium Deficiency).

FLYSTRIKE

Blowflies become attracted to any soiled skin, and lay their eggs which in hot, humid conditions can develop into maggots in less than 24 hours.

These maggots eat under the skin and release poisons, which will be fatal for the rabbit.

Signs: Often the first sign is that the rabbit becomes quiet and depressed. On closer examination the back end of the rabbit will be damp and odorous, and maggots will be seen around the vent, and under the skin, often extending halfway up the back of the rabbit.

Cause: Blowflies become attracted to any area, usually the vent, which is soiled by urine or faeces. In the hot, humid summer weather the flies lay their eggs, and these develop into fly larvae (maggots). The maggots start eating their way under the skin of the rabbit. As they do this they release an anaesthetic-like substance, so that in the early stages the rabbit may be unaware of their presence. They also release toxins into the rabbit that will cause severe shock and, ultimately, death.

Treatment: If the maggots have not had a chance to break the skin the prognosis is good. The rabbit should be thoroughly cleaned, and all the maggots and eggs removed. The area should be kept clean and dry.

If the maggots are under the skin the prognosis is poorer. If they extend over the back of the rabbit, and the rabbit is very depressed, euthanasia may be the kindest option. If treatment is tried, all the maggots must be removed. Antibiotics and cream to promote healing should be given and, if the rabbit is in shock, it will need steroid injections and fluids as soon as possible.

It is so important that the rabbit's bottom and vent are checked daily. Most at risk are those rabbits that regularly get a build-up of caecal faeces, and a diet change may be helpful *(see Sticky Bottom Syndrome)*.

FRACTURES
Rabbits are susceptible to both hind leg and spinal fractures. The most vulnerable bones are the tibia in the hind leg, and the backbone between lumbar bones 6 and 7.

Signs: Hind leg fractures will cause a sudden lameness of the affected leg. The leg will look abnormally limp. A spinal fracture may result in the sudden loss of function of both hind legs.

Cause: Many rabbits suffer from osteoporosis (weak bones). This occurs as a result of eating a low-calcium diet. Rabbits that selectively eat only certain components of their dry mix may be, unknowingly, receiving too little calcium. If the rabbit is kept in a small hutch, with no opportunity to exercise, its bones will have no chance to develop internal strength. The rabbit's natural tendency to stamp its hind feet is enough to cause a fracture of a weakened spine or hind leg.

Treatment: The rabbit should be X-rayed to determine the type of fracture. Limb fractures can be repaired surgically with the use of metal pins, or stabilised with a cast or dressing. Fractures usually take six weeks to heal, during which time the rabbit will need to be confined to a cage and rested. Complicated limb fractures that cannot be readily repaired may necessitate limb amputation. A spinal fracture can be differentiated from a 'slipped disc' on X-ray. The latter can be treated with large doses of steroids, but, if a spinal fracture is diagnosed, euthanasia is the kindest option.

G

GASTRIC STASIS

If gastric motility is reduced, food stays in the stomach for longer, and fluids are drawn out of the foodball, causing it to become solid and act as a blockage.

Signs: The rabbit becomes depressed and reluctant to move. It stops eating and no droppings are passed. The stomach may feel hard and swollen.

Cause: The gastrointestinal system should be in a constant state of movement, passing the ingesta through the system in the process of digestion. Reduced motility is usually the result of a low-fibre diet, as fibre is essential to ensure the swift passage of food through the digestive system. Stress can also slow the system down via the action of the hormone adrenaline. The ingesta spends longer in the stomach and, as the rabbit stops eating and drinking, it reabsorbs any fluid from the stomach contents into the bloodstream. The stomach contents (usually food and some hair) dry out and form a hard ball *(See Hairball)* which acts as a blockage.

Treatment: If gastric stasis and impaction is suspected the rabbit should be taken to a veterinary surgeon as soon as possible. Treatment is aimed at rehydrating the rabbit and the ingesta in the stomach by providing plenty of fluids, and with drugs that encourage the gastrointestinal system to start moving again. It may take three days of intensive nursing to resolve the problem. If the rabbit shows no sign of improvement with the drugs and nursing, the foodball can be removed surgically – but this carries a very guarded prognosis.

Fluids can be given intravenously, under the skin, or orally via a syringe. Pineapple juice can be given at the rate of 10 mls (2 teaspoons) three times a day. This will provide fluid and may help break down the impaction. The rabbit should be tempted with leafy greens, grass and dandelions to encourage it to start eating. As the condition is painful the rabbit should be given some pain relief.

The condition can be prevented by feeding a high-fibre diet (hay and green food) with reduced dry food.

H

HAEMATURIA

Haematuria is defined as blood in the urine. It can be differentiated from 'Red Urine' by a simple dipstick test.

Signs: Blood in the urine, either mixed evenly with the urine, or passed as clots at the end of urination.

Cause: The source of the blood can be either the urinary system (bladder and kidneys) or, in the doe, the reproductive system (uterus). Blood from the urinary system can be associated with infection *(See Cystitis)* or bladder stones *(See Urinary Calculi)*. Blood associated with bladder problems is usually mixed evenly with the urine, and may be accompanied by pain on urination.

Blood from the reproductive system is usually associated with blood clots, or blood passed at the end of urination. The commonest uterine (womb) disorders are endometrial hyperplasia, and uterine adenocarcinoma. *(See also Endometrial Venous Aneurysm)*.

Treatment: A dipstick test can differentiate between 'Red Urine' and true blood in the urine. If the test is positive both urinary and reproductive systems should be investigated. An X-ray of the bladder will show the presence of bladder stones *(See Urinary Calculi)* or bladder sand *(See Sludgy Bladder)*. If the bladder is normal, and there is no pain on urination, it is most likely to be a reproductive disorder which can be corrected by ovariohysterectomy.

HAEMORRHAGIC VIRAL DISEASE (HVD)
(See Viral Haemorrhagic Disease)

HAIRBALLS
An impaction of hair and food material in the stomach. These are no longer thought to be a primary condition, rather that they occur secondary to gastric stasis.

Signs: The rabbit becomes depressed and anorexic. It passes no droppings and is reluctant to move.

Cause: The rabbit's stomach should always be full of food that is being mixed with the stomach acid and enzymes and then passed onwards to the rest of the digestive system. The stomach and intestines should be in a constant state of movement. This movement stops or slows if the rabbit is on a low-fibre diet, is stressed or takes little exercise. All rabbits swallow some hair, which passes through the digestive system of a healthy rabbit without causing any problems. However, if the stomach stops moving *(See Gastric Stasis)*, the food and hair that is in the stomach dries out and turns into a matted ball that will act as a blockage. Long-haired breeds, or those in a heavy moult, are more at risk from hairballs. House rabbits that eat other fibres, such as carpet, may develop a blockage associated with these fibres.

Treatment: If a blockage is suspected, the rabbit should receive urgent veterinary attention. Treatment is aimed at rehydrating and softening the impaction and restarting the movement of the digestive system. The rabbit can be given fluids regularly by syringe. Pineapple juice is popular as it is thought to break down the mucus that holds the impaction of food and hair together. Up to 10 mls (two teaspoons) can be given three times daily. Motility drugs can be given to try and get the stomach and intestines moving again, and the rabbit should be tempted with hay, leafy greens, grass and dandelions. Pain relief will make the rabbit more comfortable. It may take up to three days to resolve the condition medically. Alternatively, the hairball can be removed surgically, but this is a risky procedure in a sick rabbit.

In order to prevent this problem, rabbits should be fed a high-fibre diet, with plenty of hay and fresh greens and wild plants, with limited dry mix. Exercise, which stimulates gut motility, should be encouraged. Longhaired rabbits, and those in a heavy moult, should be groomed regularly.

HEAD TILT

The sudden onset of a head tilt (torticollis) is a common occurrence in rabbits. This presentation may also be referred to as 'Wry Neck'. There are many causes, and it is often impossible to differentiate between them in the live rabbit, so treatment is symptomatic.

Signs: The rabbit suddenly develops a tilt of its head to one side. The twist may be so dramatic that the eye on the down side may touch the ground. The rabbit will have a poor sense of balance and may twist and spin if it is picked up. If the rabbit has had a stroke, its eyes may flick rhythmically from side to side (nystagmus).

Cause: There are various causes, the symptoms of which are identical in the live animal. Infections of the middle and inner ear are most common. 'Strokes' can also occur, and any kind of head trauma from a fight or fall can cause a head tilt. A protozoal parasite *Encephalitozoon cuniculi* produces spores (a life-stage) which migrate to the brain and cause various neurological symptoms.

Treatment: Whatever the cause, treatment is symptomatic. This usually involves a large dose of corticosteroids to reduce any swelling in the brain, and if infection is suspected, a long course of antibiotics. Recovery is slow, but if the rabbit is able to eat and drink, it should be given plenty of time to recover. The rabbit should be kept in a confined and comfortable area and handled as little as possible, because as soon as it is picked up and its feet leave the floor it will lose its balance and start spinning. The down-side eye may need bathing and eye cream if it is in contact with the ground. Even when the rabbit has recovered, a slight head tilt may persist.

HEART DISEASE

Heart disease is rare in the rabbit; however, 'heart attacks' can occur in the older rabbit.

Signs: The first sign of a heart attack may be sudden death. Rabbits with progressive heart disease may show an increased breathing rate, hind-leg weakness, anorexia and weight loss. Mouth breathing indicates severe respiratory distress, and these rabbits will have a rapid heart rate (over 200 beats/minute), and their gums may be cyanosed (blue). As the heart fails, the lungs may fill up with fluid.

Cause: Like humans, older rabbits can suffer a furring-up of the arteries associated with high blood cholesterol (arteriosclerosis). Rabbits on high-calcium diets can develop calcification of the major arteries, notably the aorta (the major blood vessel that carries blood away from the heart). When this blood vessel loses its elasticity, it is unable to respond as well to the pumping of blood by the heart, and can cause heart failure.

Rabbits that have plenty of opportunity to exercise and build up strong heart muscles are least likely to have a heart attack. A rabbit that is confined to a hutch all day with no exercise will have a weak cardiovascular system and, if stressed, the surge of the hormone adrenaline may be more than the heart can cope with, making a heart attack likely.

Treatment: Rabbits in severe respiratory distress and cyanosed will need oxygen immediately. Those with fluid on their lungs can be maintained on diuretic drugs.

HEAT STROKE
Rabbits are particularly susceptible to heat stroke. Their hutch or outdoor run should have some shelter from direct sunlight and, if kept indoors, they should be away from a window or radiator.

Signs: The first signs are those of respiratory distress (mouth breathing). As the condition progresses they become weak, depressed and incoordinated. As their temperature rises they can experience febrile convulsions.

Cause: Heat from direct sunlight or a hot radiator can raise the body temperature above 105 degrees F.

Treatment: The body temperature should be lowered by spraying the rabbit with water, immersing it in tepid water, or wrapping it in a damp towel. The rabbit may need fluids and corticosteroids to combat shock.

INCISOR MALOCCLUSION
(See Malocclusion)

INTERVERTEBRAL DISC DISEASE
Better known as a 'slipped disc'.

Signs: Depending upon the severity of the condition, the rabbit may have a hunched posture, and move its hind legs with a shuffling gait, or may have complete paralysis of the hind legs.

Cause: The intervertebral discs are like small jelly pads between each bone in the spine which act as shock absorbers. As the rabbit ages these pads become calcified and then they can move or burst upwards pushing on the spinal cord. The symptoms seen reflect the amount of damage that there is to the spinal cord.

Treatment: Treatment is aimed at reducing the pressure and swelling around the spinal cord. This involves a large dose of corticosteroids. If the rabbit is paralysed it will need intensive nursing. It should be kept clean and dry, as it is likely to suffer from urine and faecal soiling. The perineal area can be bathed and a protective moisturising cream applied.

J

JAWBONE

The rabbit has an upper (mandible) and lower (maxilla) jaw. Both are susceptible to infection (osteomyelitis) associated with tooth root infection. If the rabbit is on a low-calcium diet, the jawbone will be poorly mineralised and this can allow the teeth to move more freely in their sockets, allowing malocclusion to develop.

Signs: The lower jaw is most susceptible to infection. The lower jaw should feel smooth underneath but, if there is tooth root impaction and infection there will be bony bumps under the jaw, and abscesses can develop. Swellings in the upper jaw appear under the eyes.

Cause: A low-calcium diet can lead to poor mineralisation of the jaw. The teeth become looser in their sockets, and infection can enter and cause root abscesses.

Treatment: It is not usually possible to cure such abscesses. However, despite their size, they are generally not painful, and the rabbit can be maintained on antibiotics and repeated lancing and draining of the abscess.

KIDNEY FAILURE

Kidney failure occurs when the kidneys are no longer able to function properly. Acute failure occurs suddenly; chronic kidney failure is progressive over a longer period of time.

Signs: The rabbit drinks excessively, and subsequently urinates more. There may be urine scalding of the hind legs and abdomen. The rabbit becomes lethargic, depressed and anorexic. Rabbits with chronic renal failure lose weight and lose muscle bulk.

Cause: Acute renal failure can be caused by a bacterial infection of the kidneys. Alternatively, eating poisonous plants such as beetroot leaves and aged dock leaves can cause acute kidney damage. Chronic kidney failure generally occurs in the older rabbit as part of the ageing process. Overweight rabbits are more prone to degeneration of the kidneys.

Treatment: The rabbit needs plenty of fluids to flush the waste product urea out of the kidneys. To a certain extent this is what the rabbit is attempting to achieve by drinking more. Anabolic steroids may be given by the veterinary surgeon to try and reduce the uraemia (high blood urea), and Vitamin B will help improve the appetite. These treatments are supportive only, as the damaged kidneys are unable to repair themselves.

L

LEAD POISONING

This condition is rare but, as more rabbits are kept free-range indoors with access to household items, lead poisoning is a potential hazard.

Signs: The symptoms may be vague, initially anorexia and lethargy. Neurological symptoms such as torticollis *(See Head Tilt)*, paresis and paralysis can occur.

Cause: Lead is found in diverse sources such as old paint, curtain weights, the foil around wine bottles and the lining of photographic film cases – all of which a house rabbit would have potential access to.

Treatment: The evidence of lead poisoning can be detected on a blood test, and an X-ray of the abdomen will show the lead clearly. A course of special injections of calcium versenate is required to remove the lead from the system.

LIVER

The liver is central to the process of digestion and absorption. The most common liver condition encountered is Hepatic Lipidosis (Fatty Liver).

Signs: Anorexia, depression and dehydration.

Cause: Anorexia, even of short duration, can cause the rabbit to break down its own muscles to provide energy. This metabolism of muscle produces substances known as ketones which are excreted in the urine and breath (producing a distinct smell of 'pear drops'). The liver cells become swollen and fatty (Fatty Liver) and the rabbit will go into liver failure.

Treatment: Treatment is directed at rehydration with fluids, either intravenously, under the skin or orally. The rabbit will need to be force-fed to maintain a positive energy balance *(See Anorexia)*.

M

MALOCCLUSION

The teeth of the rabbit grow constantly throughout its lifetime, and rely on an even chewing motion to wear them down. If the teeth are, or become, out of line, they wear unevenly and overgrow.

Signs: If the front teeth (incisors) do not wear evenly they will overgrow until the rabbit is no longer able to eat or clean itself. The rabbit may begin to dribble and, if the teeth are examined, they will be seen growing in several directions. The bottom incisors may grow outwards, or upwards (into the top lip). The upper incisors may curl around into the mouth. If the tooth roots irritate the tear ducts the rabbit may develop watery eyes.

If the back teeth (molars) overgrow, the rabbit will dribble profusely and stop eating. It will develop 'Sticky Bottom Syndrome', as it will find caecotrophy painful, and the soft motions will stick to its fur around its bottom.

Cause: Incisor malocclusion may be inherited, or may occur after the teeth have been damaged by a fall, or from pulling on the cage wire. A diet low in calcium will result in poorly mineralised teeth, and a weak jawbone. This allows the teeth to move in their sockets, and to become out of position.

The molars require the side-to-side and forwards-and-backward movement of the jaw to encourage even wear. Often the diet of the rabbit does not encourage enough tooth wear; a wild rabbit would be grazing for four hours a day, whereas a pet rabbit may take 20 minutes to finish its bowl of dry food. If the molars overgrow they develop sharp spikes which grow into the tongue and cheeks causing very painful ulcers. This causes the rabbit to stop eating and dribble with discomfort.

Treatment: Incisors can be regularly trimmed or filed. However, as the teeth regrow at a fast rate this may need to be repeated every four weeks. Each time the teeth are trimmed there is a risk of the teeth shattering and becoming infected. An alternative is to have the incisors extracted. This is performed under sedation or anaesthesia, and the teeth are removed completely. Affected rabbits do very well without their incisors; they pick up their food with their lips, and chew it as normal with their back teeth.

Overgrown molars need to be trimmed and filed under sedation. This procedure will need to be repeated as the teeth regrow, sometimes as regularly as every 4-6 weeks. The provision of a high-fibre diet with plenty of hay, grass and green food will encourage normal chewing, and promote better tooth wear.

MAMMARY GLAND NEOPLASIA
Cancer of the mammary glands of the doe.

Signs: A hard swelling of one or more mammary glands.

Cause: There are two main types of mammary cancer, mammary papillomas (benign) and mammary adenocarcinomas (malignant). The latter may be associated with uterine adenocarcinoma.

Treatment: The chest of the rabbit should first be X-rayed to look for any secondary growths in the lungs. If the lungs are clear than the mammary growths can be removed surgically.

MASTITIS
An infection of the mammary glands in the doe, which usually occurs during lactation, but can be associated with pseudopregnancy.

Signs: One or more mammary glands becomes swollen, hot and painful. The doe may become anorexic, depressed and may reject her young. She may run a high temperature (up to 108 degrees F).

Cause: Mastitis can occur if the doe is kept in unsanitary conditions, where a build-up of faeces and urine will increase the risk of contamination and infection through the teats. Teat trauma, or the young biting on the nipples, will predispose a doe to the development of mastitis. The infection is caused by bacteria, most commonly *Pasteurella*, *Staphylococcus* and *Streptococcus*.

Treatment: The doe should be given antibiotics and pain relief. The affected gland can be bathed with a warm water poultice several times a day. She should be moved into a warm and clean environment. If any part of the skin over the gland becomes black and necrotic it may need surgical removal. *(See also Cystic Mastitis)*.

MIDDLE EAR INFECTION
Middle and inner ear infections are the commonest cause of head-tilting *(See Head Tilt)*. They can occur suddenly, or develop secondarily to upper respiratory tract infections.
Signs: Sudden onset of a head tilt. The head may be so twisted that the down-side eye touches the ground. The rabbit will lose its balance, and may spin or twist when it is picked up. There may be pus evident in the ear canal but, if the infection is deep in the ear, the pus may only be seen on X-ray.
Cause: The infection is caused by bacteria commonly associated with respiratory tract infections, particularly *Pasteurella* and *Staphylococcus*. These bacteria are carried in the nasal passages and can pass to the ear via the eustachian tube.
Treatment: The rabbit will need a long course of antibiotics, often for 4-6 weeks. During this time the rabbit should be confined somewhere safe and comfortable, and handled as little as possible because if it is picked up it will start spinning. If necessary the down-side eye should be bathed and treated with eye cream.

MOULTING
Rabbits moult every three months; moulting is a normal process of hair shedding.
Signs: Loss of hair, often starting at the neck, and moving across the back. The moults usually alternate between heavy and light shedding. New hair growth should be visible underneath. The skin itself should be clean; if there is any scurf or dandruff there may be concurrent *Cheyletiella* infection *(see Cheyletiella)*.
Cause: Moulting is a normal phenomenon, which has a seasonal basis.
Treatment: No treatment is necessary. However, if the rabbit appears 'stuck in moult' it can be given a vitamin tonic, or fed the plant groundsel, which will help complete the moult. It is important to remove excess hair from the hutch, and brush the rabbit, to avoid it swallowing too much hair *(see Hairballs)*. The rabbit should be fed plenty of hay to ensure the swift passage of hair through the digestive system.

MUCOID ENTERITIS
This is a serious condition and the greatest cause of death in young rabbits of 7-14 weeks old. Stress factors such as weaning, a change of diet, transportation to a pet shop or new home can all trigger disease.
Signs: Diarrhoea (often covered in mucus), lethargy, anorexia and a swollen abdomen. There may be accompanying pneumonia. Mortality is common.
Cause: The exact cause is unknown, but the symptoms are the result of an upset of the normal bacteria in the rabbit's caecum, which allow the more harmful bacteria *Clostridia* to multiply and produce toxins (poisons). Any factors that slow the movement of the caecum will allow this imbalance of bacteria to

develop. Stress associated with weaning, pet shops and mixing with other rabbits will slow the digestive system via the hormone adrenaline. A sudden change of diet, or a low-fibre diet will also allow *Clostridia* to become established.

Treatment: Sick rabbits need intensive nursing. Fluids are very important and can be given orally. A probiotic will help fill the intestines with 'helpful' bacteria. The rabbit will also need antibiotics (Tetracycline or Neobiotic are most effective), pain relief (the distended guts are painful) and drugs to stimulate the movement of the gastrointestinal system. A high-fibre diet should be offered, or the rabbit can be syringe-fed soaked rabbit pellets. An oral rehydration fluid containing electrolytes and glucose may help stimulate the appetite.

Prevention: The provision of a high-fibre diet (plenty of hay) is the single most effective preventative measure. Any dry ration should be introduced very slowly at weaning, and only after the rabbit is eating hay confidently. Stress should be minimised; when weaning, the doe should be taken away from her young, and not vice versa. Pet shops are not the best environments for baby rabbits; if a baby is bought from a pet shop it should be left quietly in its hutch for the first few days, as handling will be stressful. It should be fed plenty of hay and a small quantity of the dry food that it is accustomed to. A probiotic can be put in the drinking water over the period of weaning.

MYXOMATOSIS

An important viral disease of rabbits which is spread by insects and fleas. A vaccination is available to prevent this disease.

Signs: In the acute form the rabbit develops swellings around the eyelids, the base of the ears and the genitals. As the disease progresses the rabbit stops eating. Secondary infection with the bacterium *Pasteurella* causes pneumonia and conjunctivitis with a thick white discharge from the eyes, and is generally fatal. There is a rarer chronic form of mxyomatosis. The rabbit develops nodules on the ears, nose and paws, while remaining well in itself. These nodules eventually disappear after a period of time.

Cause: Mxyomatosis is caused by a poxvirus. It is spread by biting insects, of which the most common vector in the UK is the flea. The disease is not spread by the contact of one rabbit with another, but needs a flea to travel between the two. The incubation period (time from infection to the development of clinical signs) is 5-14 days.

Treatment: The acute form is generally fatal; it does not respond to treatment, and the kindest option is euthanasia. The chronic form can be supported with antibiotics to prevent secondary infection, and most rabbits will recover.

Prevention of this disease is the most important form of control. A vaccine is available, and is given to most rabbits annually. However, in high-risk areas, it can be repeated every six months. Vector control is also very important; the hutches can be sprayed with an environmental flea spray, and Vapona sticky fly strips or similar can be hung in the environment.

N

NAIL DISORDERS

The nail of the rabbit has a blood vessel (the quick) that runs down its centre. If a nail is torn this vessel can bleed profusely.

Signs: Blood may be found in the hutch. On close inspection one of the nails will be found to be damaged, often with the nailbed exposed. If this becomes infected it can lead to the development of osteomyelitis.

Cause: If the rabbit has overlong nails it can easily tear them in the hutch, or if it struggles when picked up. If the quick is damaged, or the nail pulled away from the nailbed, the quick will bleed.

Treatment: If the nail is still bleeding, the blood vessel should be cauterised with a styptic such as potassium permanganate. If the nailbed is proud it may need to be cut short, and a dressing applied to the foot to prevent infection. If the nailbed is infected antibiotics should be given.

NASAL DISCHARGE

Rabbits may have a nasal discharge for a variety of reasons. A white sticky discharge may be a symptom of upper respiratory infection *(See Snuffles)* or associated with dacrocystitis *(See Tear Duct Infection)*. Blood from the nose can occur following trauma, but is also a symptom of a serious viral disease *(See Viral Haemorrhagic Disease)*.

O

OBESITY

Many pet rabbits are overweight. This can lead to liver dysfunction, chronic soft stools *(See Sticky Bottom Syndrome)*, pressure sores on the hocks, and an increased risk of heart attack.

Signs: The rabbit is much heavier than its Breed Standard. Does may have a large dewlap. The rabbit may be unable to reach its anus and practice caecotrophy, and therefore have soft, smelly faeces permanently stuck to its anus. Most obese rabbits are inactive, which can predispose to the development of osteoporosis and heart disease.

Cause: Many pet rabbits are fed large quantities of concentrated dry mix and little or no hay and green food. Many rabbits also receive carbohydrate-rich treats, while taking little exercise. This is the equivalent of feeding a racehorse, then shutting it in a stable all day. Pet rabbits should have a diet based on hay, wild plants and vegetables, supplemented with a little dry mix.

Treatment: The rabbit should be dieted slowly, aiming for an average loss of 1-2 per cent of its bodyweight per week. The diet should be altered gradually towards hay and green food. Once the rabbit is eating hay, the dry mix can be removed completely. If a dry mix is fed, the rabbit should only receive small quantities at a time, and all the mix should be eaten. Some rabbits will selectively eat their favourite (and fattening) bits and leave the rest. A dry food such as Super Excel (which is made up of uniform extruded nuggets) eliminates the problem of such selective feeding.

OSTEOMYELITIS
This is the bacterial infection of bone. Infections of the jawbone are associated with tooth-root abscesses. Osteomyelitis of limb bones can be a complicating factor following a fracture.

Signs: There is secondary bone formation around the site of infection. This can result in bony swellings under the jaw, or in the upper jaw on the bridge of the nose. There may be a discharging abscess from the site of infection. Infection around a fracture site will prevent the bones from healing.

Cause: The commonest site of osteomyelitis is the jaw where it is associated with tooth-root infection. Infections of limb bones can occur after limb fracture, but also following a nailbed infection or pododermatitis *(See Sore Hocks)*.

Treatment: Osteomyelitis is almost impossible to cure. Abscesses of the jaw will need repeated lancing and flushing with an antibacterial solution. The rabbit may need long-term antibiotics. Even if the infection resolves, the bony swellings will persist. Osteomyelitis at a fracture site may impair healing to the extent that limb amputation may be necessary.

OVARIOHYSTERECTOMY
This operation, also called spaying or neutering (the female), involves the surgical removal of the ovaries and uterus. It can be done when the doe is six months old. It has positive benefits for all does. It removes the risk of developing womb cancer and other womb abnormalities. It also avoids other behaviour changes associated with the female hormones such as aggression and pseudopregnancy. A spayed doe will form a close pair-bond with a neutered male. If two does are kept together, they will also be happier if they are both spayed.

PARALYSIS
Loss of motor function and sensation of limbs.
(See Spinal Cord Injury).

PARESIS
Partial paralysis of the limbs affecting muscular movement but not sensation.
(See Spinal Cord Injury, Potassium Deficiency).

PASTEURELLOSIS

Infection by the bacterium *Pasteurella multocida* is the most common infection of the rabbit. The most well-known condition it causes is Snuffles, but it is also isolated in cases of head tilt, pneumonia, abscesses and infections of the reproductive system.

Signs: The classic symptoms of Snuffles are a heavy cold, a thick, white discharge from the nose and eyes (associated with a tear duct infection). The inside of both fore legs will be matted where the rabbit makes frequent attempts to wipe its nose. There may be an inner ear infection *(See Head Tilt)*. *Pasteurella multocida* can also cause infection of the lower respiratory tract (pneumonia and pleurisy). Abscesses can develop at distant sites, causing womb infections, testicular infections and tooth root infections.

Cause: These symptoms are caused by the bacterium *Pasteurella multocida*. Not all rabbits that contract the bacterium become ill; some can spontaneously eliminate the infection, while others become long-term carriers. The bacterium is spread by direct contact between rabbits, and can also be spread indirectly through bowls and drinkers contaminated with nasal secretions. Once in the rabbit, the bacterium can spread through the bloodstream to distant sites in the body.

Treatment: The rabbit will need antibiotics, often for an extended period of time. Some rabbits are unable to throw off the infection, but remain stabilised on the antibiotics. An antibiotic such as enrofloxacin (Baytril) is safe for long-term use. The rabbit should be maintained on a healthy diet of hay and green food to boost its immunity. Rabbits with Snuffles will benefit from intensive nursing. Their eyes and noses should be kept clear of discharge, and a mentholated vapour rub (e.g. Vick) will help clear the nasal passages and make breathing easier. Fluids are important, and can be given orally by syringe, or by an injection under the skin. Rabbits with pneumonia have a much poorer prognosis and, if their breathing is distressed, euthanasia may be the kindest option. Womb infections and testicular abscesses will require surgical removal.

PODODERMATITIS

(See Sore Hocks)

POTASSIUM DEFICIENCY

Floppy Rabbit Syndrome is seen in young rabbits that are suddenly found limp in the cage, unable to feel or to move their hind legs. The condition responds to the administration of potassium.

Signs: Young rabbits (12-14 weeks of age) are most usually affected. There is a sudden loss of feeling and movement in the hind legs.

Cause: An X-ray may be necessary to rule out any spinal trauma. Potassium is necessary for muscle movement and a lack of potassium can cause muscle weakness.

Treatment: Tomato juice is an excellent source of potassium and this can be given orally by syringe to the young rabbit. If the rabbit is not eating it should also be force-fed to maintain a positive energy balance. High doses of corticosteroids may also be given.

PSEUDOPREGNANCY

A false pregnancy will occur after any unsuccessful mating, or after an ovulation not associated with mating.

Signs: The female rabbit may start pulling out her fur and nest-building. She may become uncharacteristically aggressive. The condition lasts around 18 days.

Cause: Rabbits are spontaneous ovulators. Usually it is the process of mating that triggers ovulation and, if she is fertile, it leads to a normal pregnancy, but if it is unsuccessful, the doe will develop a false pregnancy. A doe mounting another doe can also trigger ovulation, and some does can self-induce ovulation.

Treatment: Neutering (ovariohysterectomy or spaying) is curative, and is best for any pet doe. As well as stopping further false pregnancies, it will prevent the doe suffering from womb cancer in later life. In the short term, false pregnancies can be eliminated by a hormone injection.

PYOMETRA

An infection of the uterus (womb) causing the uterus to fill up with pus.

Signs: The rabbit becomes anorexic, depressed and develops a creamy vaginal discharge. The abdomen may appear swollen.

Cause: The condition can occur in both breeding and unbred does. It may occur after an unsuccessful mating or pseudopregnancy. Un-neutered does that live with castrated bucks have an increased incidence of pyometra. The infection is caused by bacteria, commonly *Pasteurella* and *Staphylococcus*.

Treatment: Antibiotics alone will not cure the infection, and the uterus must be removed by ovariohysterectomy. This may be complicated by the fact that the uterus may have burst, allowing pus into the abdominal cavity (causing peritonitis). In these cases the prognosis is very poor. After surgery the rabbit will receive antibiotics and fluids. All non-breeding does should be neutered to prevent this condition from occurring.

QUADRIPLEGIA

A term used to describe paralysis of all four limbs. *(See Spinal Cord Injury)*. For all four legs to be affected the spinal cord trauma will be in the neck or brainstem.

RABBIT RINGS

Show rabbits are identified by metal rings that are slipped on their hind leg when they are young, and these remain permanently above the hock. They

can cut into the leg, and cause serious damage to the skin and underlying structures.

Signs: The first sign that the ring is causing problems is usually lameness. If the ring is too tight, the foot below the ring may become swollen, and the ring will cut through the skin, to the muscle. If left unattended, the whole area will become infected.

Cause: Show rabbits usually wear their rings without problems, and different ring diameters are used for different breeds, taking into account their expected adult bodyweight. However, show rabbits that are bought as pets may increase their bodyweight above the show standard, and the ring becomes tight.

Treatment: If the ring is too tight, it must be removed. Special pliers are available that enable the ring to be cut in two places, and lifted off the leg. The underlying skin should be cleaned with an antiseptic solution and, depending upon the degree of skin trauma, antibiotics, cream and dressings may be necessary. Any rabbit that is bought as a pet should have its ring removed.

RABBIT SYPHILIS
(See Vent Disease).

RED URINE
Rabbits excrete porphyrins (pigments) in the urine that colour it red. This is normal and should not be a cause for concern.

Signs: The rabbit passes urine that is orange or deep red in colour. It may be mistaken for blood in the urine *(See Haematuria)*, but a simple dipstick test can differentiate between the two conditions.

Cause: Rabbits excrete porphyrins (pigments) into the urine in varying amounts, which can colour the urine shades of orange and red. Stress can increase porphyrin excretion. The urine can also be coloured if the rabbit eats carrots, or other sources of carotene, an orange pigment which is not completely broken down and is excreted in the urine.

Treatment: This is a normal phenomenon and no treatment is necessary. True blood in the urine can be determined by a simple dipstick test and treated accordingly. (See Haematuria).

RETROBULBAR ABSCESS
An abscess develops in the eye socket behind the eye and pushes the eye outward.

Signs: The eye is pushed out from its socket. The eye itself looks a normal size, compared with glaucoma, a rare condition which makes the eye itself swell.

Cause: An abscess can develop behind the eye following a tear duct infection. The migration of a hayseed behind the eye, or a tooth root infection behind the eye socket (the orbit) can also lead to abscess development.

Treatment: This condition may respond to a long course of antibiotics. If it does not, or the rabbit is in obvious discomfort, the eye can be removed surgically.

RINGWORM

This is a skin infection caused by dermatophytic fungi. These parasitic fungi invade the outer layers of skin and hair fibres.

Signs: Dry scaly lesions on the nose and muzzle. The lesions may spread across the face around the ears and to the feet. Rabbits rarely have the typical circular rings that are seen in humans.

Cause: Ringworm is caused not by a worm, but by a fungus. There are two types – *Trichophton mentagrophytes* and *Microsporum canis*. Both can be transferred to humans and other pets. *Microsporum* has spores that fluoresce under a special ultra-violet lamp called a Wood's lamp, but special samples may need to be taken to detect *Trichophyton*.

Treatment: As the fungus lives in the hair and skin layers, it can be difficult to treat with creams alone. Antifungal washes and antifungal tablets can be given. The tablets may need to be used for 4-6 weeks to enable the ringworm spores to be eliminated from all the skin layers.

SLUDGY BLADDER

The production of urine that is so full of crystals that it is thick and cloudy in appearance.

Signs: The rabbit produces thick creamy urine. On some occasions it can be so thick it can resemble toothpaste, and may be readily mistaken for pus. The rabbit may drink more, and become depressed and anorexic. The perineal area and hind legs may become soiled with urine.

Cause: Rabbit urine is naturally alkaline, and normally contains some triple phosphate and calcium carbonate crystals which precipitate out in the urine causing its cloudy appearance. However, if there are too many crystals, the urine becomes very thick and creamy, and this can predispose the animal to the development of bladder stones *(See Urinary Calculi)* and cystitis. Diets that are high in protein and calcium predispose to crystal development. The rabbit does have an unusual calcium metabolism; whereas all other mammals have internal regulatory mechanisms that ensure that only the amount of calcium that is needed is absorbed from the diet, the rabbit absorbs all the digestible dietary calcium, and excretes any excess in the urine.

Treatment: Changing the diet can gradually alter the nature of the urine. The rabbit should receive plenty of hay, wild plants and greens, and little or none of the dry mix (which is high in protein and calcium). Alfalfa or mixes containing alfalfa should not be given, as it is very high in calcium. Most wild plants and greens are suitable; however, those with high calcium content (broccoli, watercress, kale, dandelions, parsley and spinach) should be restricted. The rabbit should be encouraged to drink to help flush the crystals from the bladder. If there is concurrent cystitis the rabbit will need a course of antibiotics.

SNUFFLES

Snuffles is the name given to the upper respiratory tract infection caused by *Pasteurella multocida* (See *Pasteurellosis*). However, short-nosed breeds may snuffle when they are eating; this is normal and associated with a shortening of the nasal passages. This snuffling sound is not accompanied by a nasal discharge.

SORE HOCKS

Rabbits with little fur cover on the back of their hocks can develop foot ulceration below their hock (the ankle).

Signs: The first sign may just be some blood around the floor of the cage. When the rabbit is examined one or both hocks may be ulcerated and bleeding.

Cause: Any rough surface (hutch floor, concrete, and wire mesh) can cause rubbing on the back of the hock. Most rabbits are protected by dense fur on the underside of the hock; however, some breeds e.g. Rex, have a sparse fur covering and are consequently prone to ulceration. Overweight rabbits, or rabbits that regularly stamp their feet, can also develop the condition. House rabbits that race around the house can similarly suffer from 'carpet burn'.

Treatment: The wounds need to be kept clean and a healing cream applied. The hocks can be dressed or covered with baby socks to give the area protection while the skin heals. The bedding in the hutch should be made as soft as possible, and an absorbent fleece-type bedding (e.g. Vetbed) can be used for house rabbits.

SPINAL CORD INJURY

Rabbits have weak spines and they can become damaged after a fall, a struggle, or even from leg stamping. The spinal cord is a large bundle of nerves that runs through the backbone carrying the nerve messages that detect sensation and control muscular movement. Any damage to the spine will result in pressure on the spinal cord and the subsequent loss of nerve function.

Signs: The sudden onset of the loss of the use of the hind legs. The clinical signs depend upon the degree of damage to the spinal cord. This may be total paralysis, where the rabbit cannot feel or move its hind legs, partial paresis where the rabbit can feel but not move its legs, or the rabbit may still maintain some ability to move but will hop awkwardly or shuffle on its hind legs.

Cause: Many rabbits have weak spines. If they are on low-calcium diets, and live confined to a hutch with no opportunity to exercise, they will develop osteoporosis (thin, brittle bones). If the rabbit struggles when it is picked up, or even if it stamps its feet in response to a fright, it may fracture its spine. The lumbar vertebrae are most susceptible to fracture around L6-L7. Thus a rabbit can be found in its hutch suddenly unable to use its hind legs.

The spinal cord can similarly become damaged in the absence of a spinal fracture. In this instance the spinal cord becomes swollen and the nerve function to the hind legs is impaired. An X-ray will show whether the spine is fractured or not. Rabbits can also suffer from slipped discs which will damage the spinal cord *(See Intervertebral Disc Disease)*. Older rabbits can suffer from degeneration of the backbone (spondylosis) which will result in the impaired function of the hind legs.

Treatment: If a spinal fracture is diagnosed on X-ray, and the rabbit has complete loss of feeling and movement of its hind legs, it is kindest to opt for euthanasia. If there is no fracture the swelling of the cord is treated with high doses of corticosteroids and diuretics. Good nursing is very important; if the rabbit is unable to move, its food and water must be easily accessible, and it must be kept clean from faecal and urinary soiling. A soft absorbent bedding such as Vetbed is ideal, and some paralysed rabbits will tolerate wearing the tiny nappies produced for newborn human babies. The perineal area can be kept clean with a gentle chlorhexidine wash, and protected with a moisturising cream (zinc and castor oil).

SPLAY LEG

This syndrome is a collection of congenital limb deformities which are evident once the rabbit leaves the nest.

Signs: The young rabbit is unable to move properly, with one or more limbs spread out.

Cause: Splay leg can be associated with hip dysplasia, bowed front legs, or incomplete development of the hip or shoulder joint.

Treatment: If mobility is severely affected, then euthanasia may be the kindest option. If only one leg is affected, then corrective surgery or leg amputation may be an option. If a hind leg is affected, the rabbit may have an increased risk of urine soiling, and will benefit from the use of absorbent bedding.

STICKY BOTTOM SYNDROME

This describes the all-too-common situation where the rabbit has soft faeces that stick to the hair around the anus. In the summer months these rabbits are at serious risk of Flystrike. This condition is not diarrhoea, but a build-up of caecotrophs (the soft faeces that the rabbit would normally re-eat).

Signs: The rabbit has a build-up of soft, and smelly faeces around its anus and tail. These faeces cake onto the fur and the rabbit is permanently dirty. The rabbit continues to produce hard droppings which it leaves around the hutch. There is a risk of Flystrike in hot, humid weather *(See Flystrike)*.

Cause: The rabbit normally produces two types of dropping: hard droppings, and soft smelly droppings that are covered in a layer of mucus. The latter are known as caecotrophs and are rich in protein and vitamins and are meant to be eaten by the rabbit (a process called coprophagy or caecotrophy). They can build up for several reasons. It may be that the rabbit is physically unable to eat them (dental problems, or is unable to reach its anus due to obesity, a large dewlap or arthritis). Rabbits on a high-protein, high-carbohydrate and low-fibre diet make too many caecotrophs, and rabbits that are overfed lose the urge to practise caecotrophy.

Treatment: Any physical reasons preventing the rabbit from reaching its anus should be treated as necessary. Obese rabbits should be encouraged to lose weight, and rabbits with large dewlaps can have them surgically reduced.

The most important treatment is dietary adjustment. The rabbit should be fed a high-fibre, low-protein and low-carbohydrate diet. This is closer to the diet of a wild rabbit, and will encourage obese animals to lose weight. There should be unlimited access to hay at all times. Wild plants can be fed such as blackberry leaves, avens, shepherd's purse and yarrow. Vegetables can be introduced slowly; one at a time until the rabbit is eating half a cup of vegetables per kg (2.2 lbs) bodyweight daily. The dry mix should be restricted, or even removed from the diet completely (as long as the rabbit is eating the hay). Any sweet treats or carbohydrates (e.g. bread) should be replaced with fruit treats. Once the rabbit is eating like one of its wild counterparts, its digestive system will function properly. It may take several months for these changes to take effect, and during this time the rabbit's bottom must be kept clean and checked daily to avoid Flystrike.

STROKE

Rabbits can suffer from 'strokes', correctly known as cerebrovascular accidents (CVAs). A blood clot becomes stuck in a small blood vessel in the brain, and there is subsequent swelling (oedema) of the brain in the affected area.

Signs: Sudden onset of head tilt, loss of balance and nystagmus (the rhythmic flicking of the eyes from side to side).

Cause: Strokes are caused by a blood clot blocking or rupturing a small blood vessel in the brain. There are, however, other causes of these symptoms *(See Head Tilt)*.

Treatment: The rabbit is given a large injection of corticosteroids to reduce the oedema in the brain. The rabbit should be kept in a confined, comfortable area and handled as little as possible. Food and water should be made readily accessible. A response to the treatment (cessation of the rapid eye movement) should be seen in 24-48 hours for a good prognosis.

T

TEAR DUCT INFECTION

The tear duct runs from the inside corner of the eye over the roots of the upper incisors and first premolar to exit out of the nostril. Any tooth root abnormalities can result in the distortion and blockage of the duct, and subsequent bacterial infection.

Signs: The rabbit has a thick white discharge from one or both eyes. The affected eye can be stuck closed with the discharge, and the conjunctiva becomes thickened and inflamed. There may also be a white discharge from the associated nostril. The fur below the eye may become matted with the discharge.

Cause: Tear duct infections are often the first sign of dental disease. The infection is usually caused by *Staphylococcus* or *Pasteurella* bacteria, which are carried in the nasal tracts of healthy rabbits, and tear duct infections often accompany upper respiratory tract infections.

Treatment: The condition may respond to antibiotics and antibiotic eye drops. However, in most cases it is necessary to flush the tear duct before the antibiotics are effective. This can be done using local anaesthetic eye drops and sedation. If the infection is severe, the flushing may need to be repeated on several occasions.

TESTICULAR WOUNDS

If two males are kept together it is likely they may start fighting when they reach sexual maturity. Often the dominant male mounts the submissive one by mounting his head. The submissive male bites the testicles of the dominant one in self-defence.

Signs: The affected testicle is bruised and swollen. In severe cases, the testicle may be eviscerated from the scrotum. If untreated, the area will become contaminated with faeces and urine and become infected.

Cause: The wounds are inflicted by another rabbit. Two male rabbits should not be kept together as they will generally start fighting once they reach sexual maturity. The one exception is if two brothers are kept together from birth and castrated as soon as possible (14 weeks) and definitely before they reach sexual maturity.

Treatment: Most testicular wounds require surgical attention. Some may just need stitching, but those involving evisceration of the testes will require castration. Antibiotics should be given if the wounds are infected.

TICKS

Ticks are parasites that may occasionally be found on outdoor rabbits. It is known that ticks can transmit Lyme Disease (Borreliosis) in dogs and humans, but no case of Lyme Disease has been reported in the rabbit.

Signs: When the tick first attaches itself to the skin it is a minute brown insect, but as it feeds from the blood and serum under the skin it swells to the size of a baked bean and is grey in colour. The mouthparts are buried in the skin, while the legs are just visible above the surface.

Cause: The most common ticks are sheep and deer ticks. These ticks will feed off any mammal and may be brought into the pet rabbit's environment by dogs, cats, and hedgehogs. The tick feeds, drops off, and awaits its next host.

Treatment: The tick must be removed very carefully as if it is pulled out it is likely that it will break and leave the mouthparts embedded in the skin which will cause an infected sore. The tick should first be suffocated by covering it with Vaseline or olive oil, and then it can be removed without resistance.

TORTICOLLIS
(See Head Tilt)

U

URINE SCALDING

The perineal area and the inside of the hind legs become soiled with urine, and subsequently the skin in this area becomes red and sore.

Signs: The underneath of the rabbit and inside its hind legs become damp and sore. There is a strong smell of urine and the fur in the area becomes soiled and matted. In hot, humid conditions flies may become attracted to the area *(See Flystrike)*.

Cause: Many factors can cause urine soiling. Most likely are disorders of the urinary tract such as cystitis, bladder stones and sludgy bladder. Kidney failure can also lead to perineal soiling.

When the rabbit urinates it lifts its back and tail in such a way that it projects the urine behind it. Mobility disorders such as arthritis, spondylitis, sore hocks and paraplegia will make such movements difficult or impossible, so that the rabbit soils itself. A loss of litter box training may be one of the first signs of arthritis in the older rabbit.

True incontinence is rare but can be associated with infection with *Encephalitozoon cuniculi* (a protozoal parasite), or spinal trauma.

Treatment: The soiled area should be bathed gently with a warm solution of an antibacterial shampoo (e.g. chlorhexidine). The skin can be protected from further soiling by the use of a water-resistant barrier cream such as zinc and castor oil. If the rabbit has mobility problems and uses a litter tray, the sides of the tray can be lowered, or the tray replaced with a low-rimmed baking-tray. House rabbits with severe mobility problems *(See Paraplegia, Quadriplegia)* will tolerate newborn-baby size disposable nappies.

URINARY CALCULI

The presence of stones in the bladder.

Signs: Blood in the urine. The rabbit may attempt to urinate frequently and show pain at the time of urination. If the stone blocks the exit of the bladder, the rabbit will be unable to urinate. A litter-trained rabbit may lose its training habits.

Cause: Rabbit urine is naturally alkaline and contains triple phosphate and calcium carbonate crystals. If these crystals build up they can form a stone or stones in the bladder. On occasion stones can also form in the kidneys. The formation of stones is most likely if the rabbit is on a high-calcium and high-protein diet, and does not drink much.

Treatment: The rabbit is X-rayed to look for the presence of stones. Any stones in the bladder can be removed surgically. After the stones are removed the rabbit is given antibiotics and the protein and calcium content of its diet reduced *(See Sludgy Bladder)*. It is not easy to make the urine less alkaline, but ascorbic acid (Vitamin C) can be added to the drinking water at a dilution of 200mg/litre. Soluble Vitamin C tablets are readily available from a chemist.

UTERINE ADENOCARCINOMA
Womb cancer is the commonest cancer of the rabbit. It is estimated that it may affect up to 80 per cent of does over the age of six years.

Signs: Does can become affected from as early as two years of age. Intermittent blood in the urine is the first symptom, and blood clots may be passed at the end of urination. It is difficult to distinguish this condition from endometrial hyperplasia at this stage. The doe may become more aggressive, and as the growth enlarges it may cause discomfort, leading to anorexia and an increased respiratory rate. The cancer can spread to the mammary tissue, liver and the lungs.

Cause: This condition may follow on from endometrial hyperplasia. The cancerous change is thought to be associated with falling oestrogen levels as the doe ages.

Treatment: The growth is often palpable when the abdomen is felt. Ovariohysterectomy (removal of the womb and ovaries) is curative if done before the cancer has spread.

Other rarer causes of a swollen womb are Hydrometra, when the womb fills up with watery fluid, and Endometrial Venous Aneurysm, when the womb fills up with blood. Ovariohysterectomy is curative for both these conditions.

VENT DISEASE
Also known as rabbit syphilis, this disease causes lesions on the genitals, and occasionally on the face. The majority of cases are sexually transmitted.

Signs: Crusty lesions primarily on the genitalia, but these may spread to the face as the rabbit cleans itself. The lesions begin as vesicles (blisters) that burst and crust over. Affected rabbits are not clinically ill.

Cause: The disease is caused by a spirochete called *Treponema cuniculi*. The organism is transferred by direct contact at mating, or by a doe to her young at parturition (birth). The incubation period (the time between infection and development of clinical signs) is at least eight weeks, and some rabbits can carry the organism for months before the disease is triggered by stress.

Treatment: This condition is one of the only times when penicillin should be given *(see Antibiotic Induced Diarrhoea)*. All affected and in-contact rabbits should be treated at the same time.

VIRAL HAEMORRHAGIC DISEASE (VHD)
VHD is caused by a calici virus, which was first identified in China in 1984, and spread across Europe to reach Britain in 1992. In most cases infection is fatal.

Signs: Sudden death, often proceeded by convulsions and nose bleeding. Less acute cases may be anorexic, breathless and lethargic before they convulse and die. Some cases may just have a period of lethargy and anorexia before they recover. However, recovered rabbits are more prone to develop secondary infections such as 'Snuffles' and diarrhoea.

Cause: VHD is caused by a calici virus, which once in the body causes haemorrhages in many organs, particularly the lungs and kidneys. The virus is spread between rabbits via their nasal secretions but can also be spread indirectly via insects, birds, rodents, people and their clothing. The virus may have been brought to Britain via cross-Channel traffic.

Treatment: Positive control measure is vaccination, and a vaccine is available that can be given to rabbits from 10-12 weeks of age and repeated annually.

WARTS
These are small crusty lesions on the skin surface.

Signs: These lesions are generally found on the ears and the eyelids. They are usually 2-3 mm in diameter and are raised and crusty.

Cause: They are caused by a virus *(Shope Papillomavirus)* which is transmitted to pet rabbits from wild rabbits by insect vectors.

Treatment: No treatment is necessary as these warts are of no clinical significance. However, surgical removal is possible if any are in such a place as to irritate the rabbit.

WOMB CANCER
(See Uterine Adenocarcinoma).

WORMS
Occasionally long, thin thread-like worms will be seen on the rabbit's droppings.

Signs: Small white worms (5 mm long) may be seen on the droppings or stuck to the rabbit's bottom.

Cause: These worms are pinworms *(Passaluris ambiguous)*. They do not cause disease in the rabbit. The adults live in the large intestine, and shed eggs in the faeces.

Treatment: Treatment is not entirely necessary, as these worms do not cause disease. However their presence can be reduced by using a wormer such as Panacur (containing the drug fenbendazole).

WRY NECK
This term describes the condition where the rabbit's head becomes suddenly twisted to one side *(See Head Tilt).*

X-RAYS

Most veterinary surgeries possess X-ray machines and are able to take X-rays (radiographs) and develop them instantly. X-rays can be a useful diagnostic aid in the investigation of a disease. Most rabbits should be sedated or anaesthetised for X-ray as Health and Safety regulations insist that staff using the X-ray machine are not exposed to the X-ray beam, and should therefore not hold the patient on the X-ray plate.

YEAST INFECTION
(See Candidiasis).

ZOONOSES

Zoonoses are those diseases that can be transmitted to humans from animals. Potential zoonotic diseases from rabbits are Cheyletiella, Fleas, Ringworm, and Salmonella. The protozoal parasite *Encephalitozoon cuniculi* could be a risk to an immunosuppressed person. *Cheyletiella* causes a transient itchy skin rash, whereas Ringworm produces classic circular skin lesions. Rabbits with such infections should be treated appropriately and handled carefully until they are cured. A bite or scratch from a rabbit can become infected, particularly if the rabbit is carrying *Pasteurella*. Any bite or scratch should be washed immediately with an antiseptic solution.

CHAPTER 10

THE RABBIT COAT

1. The fur groups
2. Judging sections
3. Colour

Cry Baby Bunting
Daddy is gone a hunting
Just to get a rabbit skin
To wrap the Baby Bunting in!
(Old nursery rhyme)

The rabbit coat is made up of four types of hair:

- Primary Guard Hairs. These are stout, straight and even in diameter, except where they increase to a maximum near the tip before tapering off to a fine point.
- Straight Secondary Guard Hairs. These are thinner, having pronounced spear-like tips.
- Crimped Secondary Guard Hairs. These are thinner and wavy.
- Wool Hairs. These are fine, evenly crimped and uniform throughout the length of the hair; they make up most of the rabbit's coat.
  The ratio of guard hairs to wool hairs varies between 20 to 1 and 50 to 1. The number of the different guard hairs decreases from the crimped form of the secondary guard hairs to the straight form and to the less numerous primary guard hairs.

Rabbit breeds

1. THE FUR GROUPS
Rabbit fur can be classified into five general groups:

- Normal Fur – the coat one expects to see on a rabbit. It has long guard hairs and a dense undercoat.

- Rex coat – this looks plush and is the result of a decreased rate of hair growth making the coat shorter than the normal. The primary guard hairs are lacking and the secondary guard hairs are thinner than normal, being only a little longer than wool hairs, rather than being noticeably longer. This can vary, however, and it is possible to find Rex coats with guard hairs projecting above the wool hairs, although most of the hairs should be of the same length.

- Astrex – this is a waved Rex. A problem with this variety is that the full extent of waving may not be apparent for perhaps a year. This type of coat occurs periodically in a fair number of breeds. I have seen a wavy-coated New Zealand White and I had such a coat appear on a French Lop.

- Opossum – this is a long-haired type of Rex which possesses a stiff coat evenly ticked with silvering. The tips of the Rex guard hairs are curled and this curling is exaggerated in longer-haired Rex. The curling is shown up by the white secondary guard hairs of the Opossum, standing above the wool hairs and curving slightly in all directions. I know of only one breeder of this type of rabbit in the UK, who struggles along doing his best to perfect this very striking coat.

- Satin – like the Rex coat, this is also a mutation. Hairs of the coat are thinner than usual with a very shiny, glass-like surface. All hair types are affected, giving the coat a soft, silky texture which makes the coat colour appear darker than usual because the pigment granules within the hair seem to be flattened and packed closely together. This is an American discovery.

- Angora – this coat is extra-long due to growth of the hair beyond the normal period. Well-wooled Angoras are the result of a long period of selective breeding. European Angora has a slightly thicker hair; English type is extremely fine. There are other long-haired types of rabbit, the Cashmere Lop, the Swiss Fox etc., and they are no relation to the Angora. If the presence of Angora is suspected in a breed, one only need look at the base of the coat nearest the skin and the tell-tale slight wave or crimp will appear.

- Fancy – this coat differs from a fur rabbit. It is usually smooth and lies close to the skin. Because of its varying colours it is known as 'fancy'.

2. JUDGING SECTIONS
Rabbits are also divided into group sections for exhibition purposes, for example:

- Giant Breeds
- Medium Breeds

110

- Small Breeds
- Dwarf Breeds.

There are breeds with different hair structures, such as Rex, Angora, Satin etc., and each breed has its own Standard of Perfection, usually 100 points. Points are awarded at shows using an agreed scale that has been stipulated as the ideal to be aimed for in that particular breed (see Glossary).

The European Confederation are now producing a Standard of all breeds with a common Standard for use internationally. The Standard Commission has been working on this for the past four years. The biggest hurdle has been weight, because Germany and Switzerland breed larger rabbits than elsewhere, and they are very good rabbits too. In the UK the same breeds tend to be smaller, although the breeders there excel in breeding wonderful coats.

I read an American book some time ago written by a Judge of Miss World and it amused me immensely because it could have matched up with the Rabbit Standard, except for 'Facial Expression', 'Grace of Bearing' and the inevitable question 'What is your aim in life?'. It reads:

Construction of Head	15 points
Eyes	10 points
Hair (Rabbit gets 20)	5 points
Nose and Mouth	10 points
Facial Expression	10 points
Torso	10 points
Legs	10 points
Arms	10 points
Hands	10 points
Grace of bearing	10 points

3. COLOUR
This is a very thorny subject and it causes more bad feeling between judges and exhibitors than any other aspect of rabbit breeding. I have often wished that the spectrum of coat colours would diminish. For example, the blue rabbits encompass a whole range of blues; although the range of the colour blue is about 45 shades, rabbits are limited to dark, medium, light, powder-blue, lavender-blue, slate-blue, sky-blue etc. Judging a blue rabbit can be a hazardous business. The male judge has a very different idea of blues from that of the female judge. I always like to point out to some tetchy judge that men have a 12 per cent defect in colour vision while that of the woman is 1 per cent.

The lilac rabbit no longer has the Standard description of pinky dove with a mixture of bronze and pinky feathers on the breast. The UK lilac rabbit lost this lovely colour when the breeders bred out all traces of brownish tint. The Dutch breeders have the Govwanar, which is truly lilac, and they are experts in colouring – better than any other country.

In the UK we cannot leave well alone and every imported rabbit, no matter what the original colour, sooner or later undergoes a change, either by having its coat or its colour changed, sometimes with dire results. Type tends to suffer in the process and to me there is no more wonderful colour than that of the wild rabbit in full coat.

It should be noted that black fur can also turn greyish if there is a copper deficiency in the diet.

DID YOU KNOW?

The rabbit coat also has its place in high fashion. Some colours fade with age or if left in full sunlight. Blacks become rusty, white loses its clarity, browns and tans likewise. But it can be sheared, dyed and imprinted to represent any other animal and coney fur has been wrapped around many a famous person. When the Queen Mother married in 1923, friends were advised that because of wartime austerity there should be "no expensive fur gifts please, only squirrel or rabbit". Her husband, George VI, always wore a rabbit skin cap when gardening at Royal Lodge. Princess Mary, the daughter of George V and Queen Mary, was given a magnificent coat of Blue Beveren rabbit fur on the occasion of her wedding to the Earl of Harewood. Brigitte Bardot had three rabbit coats from Dior: Blue, Pink and Orange.

Now for a tale of a breeder's attempt at making himself a pair of mittens from rabbit skin:

Of the skin he made him mittens
Made them with the fur side inside
With the skin side outside.
He, to get the warm side inside
Put the inside skin outside.
He to get the cold side outside
Put the warm side inside
That's why he put the outside inside
Why he put the skin side outside
Why he turned them inside outside
All it needed was a little know-how!

Anon
From *A Modern Hiawatha*

CHAPTER 11

THE BREEDS

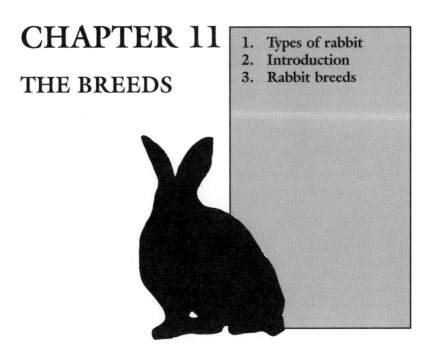

1. TYPES OF RABBIT
Remember, all rabbits stem from the wild one.

- Pronolagus: Has longer tail than any other rabbit – four species.
- Nesolagus: Small, mottled rabbit from Sumatra – now very rare.
- Pentolagus: Dark-coloured species from Liuku Islands – Japan.
- Silvilagus: 15 species – resembles European type – varies in size with short to very short tails, e.g. American Cottontail.
- Caprolagus: Dark-coated rabbit found in Nepal, Assam, Western India, also known as the Bristly rabbit.
- Brachylagus: West/North America.
- Romerolagus: Small – almost black – looks like a rat with little or no tail and short ears, found on slopes of Popocatapetl, Mexico.

2. INTRODUCTION
There are 50 known breeds and each breed comes in its 'infinite variety' with variations of colours, coat, textures, sizes, dwarfs and so on. By comparison the wild rabbit remains the same – flat-coated, fairly small with agouti colours, a mixture of blue, black and yellow. The first variations in colour, as far as I know, were black, white and piebald. In the 17th century, we hear of the silvered variety. Gerald Markham (see Section One) gave a good description of the first

silver, which from his account was a real fur-coated rabbit. The Piebald, also known as the Brabant, was the ancestor of our very well-known Dutch rabbit. In the 17th century, Sir John Evelyn gave a description of 'Yellow' rabbits seen in Europe. In 1814 Darwin discovered 'black and white conies' in the Falkland Islands. An islander told him that these two colours produced grey rabbits.

The 19th century saw the burgeoning of rabbit breeding. 'Lop-eared sorts' were extremely popular, so much so, in fact, that it was named 'King of the Fancy', a title it retains to this day. Unfortunately for the Lop, its ears became all-important and the length and width were all that mattered. The poor Lop was subjected to all sorts of cruel practices to gain the longest and widest ears, while its body did not matter, and so it became deformed in type (see Judging Lops). In 1997, it made the Guinness Book of Records with ears twenty-eight-and-a-half inches long.

In the latter part of the 20th century, new varieties came along: the Dutch, the English, the Black and Tan, the Belgian Hare and the English Silver. The English Silver was very different from Markham's Silver Coney, as it was smooth-coated with a fly-back coat (that is, if it is stroked against the way the coat lies, it naturally flies back to its original position). There was also a large yellow and white rabbit, and in 1892 the tri-colour. This was the forerunner of the Japanese or Harlequin and, more recently, the tri-coloured Dutch.

The origins of the English Pole are completely lost. It has been suggested that its origins are in Poland, which is pretty doubtful. I have seen the odd wild white rabbit and it could be almost a twin of the Pole, for it looks like the same, small, very alert little animal (white rabbits are, in fact, very rare in the wild).

The Chinchilla was bred in France in 1913 and arrived in Britain in 1919, closely followed by the Rex in 1920. The Rex really caused a stir because its coat was so unusual (it was said to be a mutation from syphilitic rabbits). The next bombshell was the arrival of the Netherland Dwarf in 1940, which has proved to be extremely popular and has made a world-wide impact. Many other breeds have now been dwarfed and the colour range is truly extensive. Giant breeds, meanwhile, have more or less gone out of fashion.

The other breeds with coat variations are the American Satin, Angora, Astrex, Opossum, and two extinct breeds – the Hooded Muscovy and the Swan. The Muscovy, or Moscow rabbit, is long extinct and is described below under 'hooded rabbit'.

Of all breeds of rabbit, I love the wild rabbit best of all. It has a wonderful colour, perfect symmetry of body and, dare I say it, more intelligence than the domestic rabbit!

In this chapter, for the sake of precision, I have used metric and imperial measurements where appropriate for each breed, as rabbits from many different countries are included. A simple conversion chart can be found at the back of the book.

DID YOU KNOW?
A South American rabbit which is red with a white head may have been a chance mutation. In the late 1960s I was informed of a wild black rabbit with a white head which was seen in North East Scotland, in Thurso, Caithness.

3. RABBIT BREEDS

ALASKA

The origin of the Alaska is possibly in Switzerland or Germany. Its ancestry is Himalayan, Argente and Dutch. The creator is not known. This is one of few truly black rabbits, with a coat like polished jet. In England it was known as the Nubian. It became extinct in the UK and was reintroduced by Peter Townson from Belgium in 1972. It is a dual-purpose rabbit, kept for fur and meat. Its weight is 7-8 lbs and it is thickset and dumpy. The coat is intensely black and dense, with a wonderful sheen. This rabbit was used to create the black Rex. There was also a white Alaska, now long extinct. I do not know which came first, although Alaska seems an odd name for the blackest rabbit!

AMERICAN

As its name states, this is an American creation, credited to Lewis Salisbury of California. The first rabbits were blue, and then some breeders began to get whites in their litters from the blues which were originally from various crosses. Two colours were recognised – blue and white. The white played an important part in the creation of the New Zealand White. They were mandolin-shaped with a broad, meaty back. They weigh 9-10 lbs and the coat is very dense and thickly interspersed with strong guard hairs. The Whites are pure white over the entire body, the Blues are a rich, clear, dark, slate-blue all over.

ANGORA

This rabbit is also known as the St Innocent, or the 'Turkey' rabbit and it is not a fur-coated rabbit, but a wool-coated one (See Glossary). Of all the breeds, it has more tales surrounding its history than any other. Some say it originated in Asia Minor and was called Angora because its long silky coat was akin to that of the Angora Goat. It has also been alleged that it came from the province of Angora in Turkey and thus was known as the Angora Rabbit or the 'Turkey' Rabbit. However, most old writers say it is definitely English in origin (where it was bred extensively).

Angora rabbit c. 1800.

The Angora in moult c. 1800.

It is recorded that the Angora appeared in France in 1723, introduced by Maitre Teannot, and in Germany in 1766 by a breeder called Von Meyers, and soon it spread all over Europe. In 1874 in Germany the *Manual of Breeding the Angora Rabbit of England* was published. This English Angora was a small rabbit, of about 5lbs in weight. It resembled a snowball, although its wool was very silky and extremely fine in texture. It was considered too fine for commercial use so it was crossed, in about 1906, with the French Blanc de Bouscat.

At the end of the 17th century in Europe there was only one type of rabbit – the common farm rabbit. Frere Espanet, a monk, said he could transfer any farm rabbit into one with an angora coat. It was well known that ponies used in the mines, never coming into daylight, developed long, straight, woolly coats and that all that was needed to put an angora coat on a common rabbit was to breed them in warm dark places. The old colours were white, the Siberian with a black nose, blue fawns and silvers. There was also a piebald grey and white; now there are several colours.

The European Angora is a more massive rabbit, not so fine in wool but of a terrific density, producing about 1 kilo of wool in a year, which is almost double that of the English variety. The wool used to be plucked by hand but now is clipped or sheared.

ARGENTE CHAMPAGNE

This is the oldest and best known of the silver rabbits. Gervase Markham described it in 1631 and it is mentioned in an encyclopaedia of 1715. It was introduced into Britain in 1920 although, strangely enough, the French give the country of origin as England. Now we also have the blue, creme and brown. The Argentic creme is the smallest of the silvers. It is self-coloured in the nest and begins silvering from 6-8 weeks, the process being completed in 6-7 months. The newest colour is Noir (black).

Argente Champagne – the silver rabbit (Rice).

116

ASTREX

This was a rough-coated Rex created by Mrs De Ville Mathers in 1933. There were no guard hairs and the fur was short and curled all over and looked like a Broad Tail. It was a recognised breed, but it did not seem to breed true and can now be said to be extinct. A mutation of the Astrex appears periodically in other breeds.

BEAVER

Now extinct, this was a cross between a Beveren and a Havana. It had really lovely fur, which was very lustrous, dense and silky. The creator is unknown.

BEIGE

This no longer exists in the UK but it does, however, exist in Europe and Natal, South Africa. It is a stoutly-built but finely-boned rabbit. The fur is dense and silky, and is 1-1.5 ins long. Its colour is like light sea-sand and it goes right down to the skin, where it is faintly ticked with slate-blue. The top colour is light and sandy flecked and is carried deep down on the flanks with blue shadings which are also present on the muzzle, ear edges and ear bases. The tail is beige on top and blue underneath, and the belly is beige with deeper blue shadings; the eyes and nails are brown.

BELGIAN HARE

As the name suggests, this rabbit originated in Belgium and was bred by selection from Giant Rabbits. It was named Hare because its original colour resembled that of the wild hare. At one time it was a mixture of a sandy colour with black, and the belly was creamy white; the head was nice and square. It was imported into the UK in 1874 by the Brothers Lamb, who were importers of livestock from the Low Countries.

Most of the hares around this time were introduced into warrens. More were crossbred with Lops and Giant Rabbits for meat purposes. It was then a utility rabbit. The modern Hare is very different; it is an elegant, showy, rich deep tan rabbit, which is quite a different colour. It should be noted that in Europe the Hare is of a heavier build. In the last two to three years we have seen two new colours – Black and Tan from Holland, and White with black eyes from Belgium.

A point of interest about the Belgian Hare is that, long ago the does often threw self-reds in their litters. It would be interesting to be able to identify these, perhaps as either the Old English Red or the Big Red.

BEVEREN

This is another Belgian breed. This rabbit has caused great confusion because there were two main blue breeds, the Beveren and the St Nicholas Blue. They were the same type but had one difference; the St Nicholas had a white blaze on the face, which was finally bred out. The bone of contention is the question of which came first. A Standard was drawn up in 1902 but this did not clear up the problem, for in 1905 and 1906 Beverens were being shown carrying the white blaze. Then two classes were provided at shows: the Beveren with Blaze and the Beveren without Blaze.

Finally it became the all-blue Beveren. This was imported into Britain in 1915, and even then there were two types! A small one was known as the Brabacon and the other was the Giant Beveren. In 1919 blacks appeared, in the late 1920s the white appeared, and in the 1930s the brown also appeared. By this time the smaller Brabacon had disappeared. The white Beveren was bred in three varieties: pink-eyed, black-eyed and opal-eyed (greeny yellow). The year 1980 saw a new colour – lilac.

The weight of the Beveren is not below 7lbs, the fur is very dense, silky and lustrous, and is not less then one inch in length, not more than one-and-a-half inches. The colour is a clear lavender-blue.

There was also the pointed Beveren, formerly the Pointed Fox, which became extinct for many years. It was re-created in 1984 by H. Nicholson.

BLACK AND TAN (NOIR AND FEU)

This breed originated in England and was found on an estate in Brailsford, near Derby. In 1884, the owner of this estate, Mr Cox, put a large number of different rabbit breeds into his warren and, from some unknown crossing, the first Black and Tans appeared. They still appear in a wild state in Scotland. In 1891 a Standard was drawn up and the National Black and Tan Club was formed. Next came the Blue and Tan, a crossing of a Black and Tan buck with a sooty fawn short-eared doe. This doe is said to have come from a tortoiseshell Dutch Rabbit. Chocolate and Tan appeared in 1922 and Lilac and Tan in 1933.

The Black and Tan was introduced into France in 1894 and to Switzerland in 1900. It is a very popular show rabbit in Europe. The weight is 5.5-6 lbs.

BLANC DE BOUSCAT

This breed originated in France in 1906 and was bred by Mme Dulon. It is the result of several crossings between the Argente Champagne, the Angora and the Flemish Giant. It is well known as a meat and fur rabbit. It was originally known as the Ermine rabbit and was first shown in Paris in 1910. It is an excellent meat rabbit and a prolific breeder, with litters usually of 7-9 youngsters. When the youngsters are 8 months old the coat is absolutely superb: soft, dense, long, silky and supple, with a frosty, gleaming sheen. It almost rivals Angora wool for fineness. The weight is 6.5-7 lbs. It should be noted that it is now on the French list of breeds at risk and is very rare in the UK.

BLANC DE CHAUNY

This was another fine breed but is now extinct. It was bred principally for its pelt which was large, snow-white and in much demand by the fur trade. The pelt also took easily to dyeing and imprinting. It has been suggested that it had been bred from the Argente Champagne, which would have given it the white pelt with a black/brown eye.

BLANC DE HOTOT

This is a French breed from patterned rabbits of Dutch and bi-coloured Butterfly breeds. It is a thickset, snowy-white rabbit with bold, brownish-black eyes. A narrow, even black band, 2-3 mm in width, surrounds each eye, giving the rabbit the appearance of wearing spectacles. The body fur is very dense and silky and gleams like frost.

It is interesting to note that Mme Dulon had almost 600 crosses before she was finally satisfied. It was introduced into the USA in the 1980s and is now named the Egyptian or Pharaoh rabbit.

There was also a Giant Black Hotot which is now extinct. The Blanc de Hotot has recently been rexed by Herr Eikern of Switzerland. It has also appeared as a dwarf breed.

BLANC A L'OURAL
This was a large white rabbit, created by M Petrequin of France. It was last heard of in French Standards of 1927. It was of Albino type with dense, lustrous fur and was pink of eye. Its weight was 4-5 kg and it is now extinct.

BLANC DE TERMONDE
This is a Belgian-bred cross of Flemish Giants and Beveren. It is a large rabbit with a rectangular body and large ruby eyes. The short silky coat is very brilliant and really snowy white. It is an excellent meat rabbit which can produce 2 kg of meat at four weeks.

BLANC DE VENDEE
This is a really beautiful dual-purpose rabbit for meat and fur. It is a crossing of Beveren and Angora and was bred by Mme Douillard of France in 1911. An albino was found in a litter of blue Beverens and was later crossed with the Angora to produce this breed. The fur is very dense, close, short and silky. Its eyes are rose pink and its weight is 3.5-4 kg. It was officially recognised in the Breed Standard of 1924.

BOURBONAIS GREY
This is a French breed, created by P. Champonnaud from grey rabbits. It is a very rare breed and is very meaty, firmly muscled and compact. The colour has an even, dark-grey tint. The coat is formed by different tints, one on top of the other. The basic colour is slate blue followed by an intermediate light brown and guard hairs are dark grey-tipped black. The eyes are brown and are encircled by a pale grey ring. Its weight is 4-5 kg.

BROWN CHESTNUT OF LORRAINE
This is a French breed and is quite rare. It was bred by Charles Kaufmann from wild rabbits and the Black and Tan. It is a small rabbit, but is one of the loveliest I have ever seen. It is a well-rounded little rabbit with a chestnut brown fur. This colour is composed of layers of different shades. An intermediate coat of orangey brown gives brilliance to the top coat, which is a lovely chestnut colour sprinkled with black-tipped guard hairs. The whole coat is very short and dense and the ears are edged with black. If the intermediate colour lacks a good orangey brown shade it will look more like a wild rabbit in colour. The weight is 1.5-2 kg.

CALIFORNIAN
This is truly a 'made in USA' rabbit, bred by a Mr West who was a furrier as well as rabbit breeder and judge. He realised there was a need for a good meat rabbit with usable pelt. Californians were first shown at an American breeders' convention in 1923. At first the rabbit was known as the Ermine, or Cochinellas, but this was soon changed to the present name Californian. It was bred from crossed New Zealand Whites, Chinchilla and Himalayan. The latter gave it the characteristic markings of coloured nose, ears, feet and tail which were to be as black as possible. It is primarily

a first-class meat rabbit, being well rounded and firmly fleshed on fine bone. The fur has a dense undercoat, with coarser guard hairs of medium length. The breed was imported into the UK from the USA in 1950s and made its first appearance at the Bradford Championship show in 1961. The type is still the same, with an addition of chocolate and lilac coloured points.

CHAUDRY
This is a French commercial breed bred by M Wiltzer, one-time President of the Aviculture de France Association. It is a hybrid created from all the white French breeds and, as one breeder put it "It is just a salad of white rabbits!" The Blanc de Hotot and Blanc de Vienna were not included as they are impure whites. The Chaudry has the ideal meat formation with a minimum weight of 4 kg. Youngsters reach carcass weight of 1.5 kg at 10 weeks. The does are prolific breeders with litters of a minimum of seven youngsters.

CHIFOX
This is an English breed from a crossing of Chinchilla and Fox; the creator was T. Leaver though the breed is no longer in the UK. It was produced in all colours and was an excellent fur breed. The fur was 2.5 ins long and extremely dense so that the skin was invisible. It should be noted that it is now making a comeback.

CHINCHILLA
This is of French origin and was bred by M Dybowski. Its ancestry is wild rabbits crossed with the Himalayan and the Beveren. It was first exhibited in 1913 and arrived in the USA and the UK in 1919. When it appeared on the show bench, it caused great interest. There is also a German version, the Large Chinchilla, which is double the weight of the original Chinchilla which is 5.5-6.5 lbs. It is short, cobby, plump and finely boned. The fur is exquisitely soft, fine and dense with the length of coat 1-1.5 ins. It was bred to resemble the real Chinchilla. In colour, the fur is dark blue at the base, and its intermediate colour is pearl, with a narrow black edging. The dark blue base colour is wider than the pearl and the top colour is grey with bright black hair ticking.

Chinchilla. (The inset shows colour rings when the fur is blown). From the Whippell Collection, reproduced from Fur & Feather, 1928.

RABBIT BREEDS

Angora.

Belgian Hare.

Black And Tan.

RABBIT BREEDS

Chinchilla.

Dutch.

English Silver.

RABBIT BREEDS

Silver Fox.

Harlequin.

Havana.

Himalayan.

English Lop.

Netherland Dwarf Lop.

124

Cashmere Lop.

Netherland Dwarf.

New Zealand White.

RABBIT BREEDS

New Zealand Red.

Polish

Rex.

126

RABBIT BREEDS

Smoke Pearl Rex.

Satin.

Dwarf Lionhead.

127

Typical scene at a rabbit show.

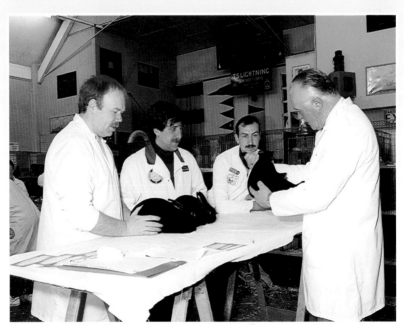

Each rabbit is judged to evaluate how closely it conforms to the Breed Standard.

In Holland there is the Apoldro which is a brown, or Havana, Chinchilla bred by A. Cornelissen de Beer. There is also a brown Chinchilla that was bred in France in 1952 and a blue and an iron-grey bred in Germany in 1935. The breed has also been rexed. The Chinchilla Giganta was an English creation, bred by Chris Wren from Flemish Giants and Chinchillas. Other large chinchillas are: The German Grose Chinchilla, 12 lbs; The American Heavy Chinchilla, 10 lbs; American Giant Chinchilla, 15 lbs. All have the same coat colouring and now the French have the brown Chinchilla rexed.

CINNAMON
This is a US rabbit created by Ellis Housman. Its ancestry is unknown. It is a well-developed rabbit and tapers slightly from rump to shoulders. The weight is 4.3 kg The fur is very thick and dense, and not too soft or too coarse. The colour is rust or cinnamon, with an even, smoke-grey ticking across the back, blending into smoke-grey on the flanks and darkest on the belly. The undercoat colour is orange. There is also a distinct butterfly smut on the nose and also small, but distinct, eye circles.

DEILENAAR
This breed originated in Holland in 1940 by crossing the Belgian Hare, the New Zealand Red and the Chinchilla. The creator was G.W. Ridgehof. It is a short, thickset rabbit with a powerful, almost invisible, neck. The weight is 2.5-3.5 kg and the fur is very dense and close. The top colour is a warm reddish-brown with strong wavy ticking and resembles that of the Hare. The chest is a very rich red. The under-colour is blue and the ears have black lacing like that of the Hare. This is a really beautiful rabbit.

DUTCH
This has a most fascinating history. It is actually descended from an ancient breed, the Dwarf Brabancon. It was purely a meat rabbit of weight 7-9 lbs, known in France as the Nicard, and is now one of the most popular breeds in Britain. In 1894, Van der Snickt stated in an article in *Chasse et Peche* that the Brabancon Dwarfs were arriving in London in large consignments from Ostend every week; however, English breeders had already, before 1930, named this rabbit the Dutch.

Black and Blue Dutch. From the Whippell Collection, reproduced from Fur & Feather, 1931.

FUR & FEATHER

Mr Copeman, founder of the Dutch Rabbit Club, wrote to Van der Snickt in November 1894. He had been living in London for five years and had the habit of examining each consignment of rabbits that arrived from Ostend. He had found and bought one which had the white markings he had been looking for, with the body neatly divided exactly in two, black and white. In the same year, Van der Snickt wrote "the English are making show rabbits with certain white markings". These were a regular marked blaze of white on the face, with the front half of the rabbit white, and the other half black with white feet. In 1899, Van der Snickt tried to set out the differences between the English Dutch Rabbit and the Brabancon, and he drew up a Standard which was accepted. His rabbit was a much larger animal, with spoon-shaped ears held in a V-shape. The white blaze on the face was narrow, starting on the forehead and encircling the nose, throat and neck, which was long, like a collar.

In Britain a battle had raged over new and old markings (the old style is the style to which we are now accustomed). In 1890, the steel-grey appeared, known as the Palmer, which was the result of crossing a self-steel wild doe and a black Dutch buck (steel means mixed grey and black hairs). The breed is now recognised in seven different colours.

The weight of the Dutch in the UK is 4.5-5 lbs, but the breed is larger and heavier in Europe.

TRI-COLOUR DUTCH

This really originated in Holland, unlike the Dutch, and was bred from marked rabbits, mainly the original Japanese. It is now known as the Harlequin in the UK, but as the Japanese elsewhere (the name was changed during the last war). It has been in existence for over a century. It has an odd pattern of Dutch markings superimposed with a harlequin, or Japanese, pattern. The head and face pattern follows that of the Dutch, with the characteristic white blaze on face; the black half of the rabbit should be banded as regularly as possible in orange and black. The fur is thick with plenty of undercoat. This rabbit has a small but very dedicated following.

ENGLISH BUTTERFLY

The ancestry of the English Butterfly is common spotted rabbits (warren rabbits mixing with others of different colours which produced litters with spotted, or rather different-coloured, patches) with a smut. Delamer in his book *Pigeons and Rabbits* (1850), gives a description of the Blue Butterfly Smut which was then considered to be a most valuable rabbit. It is thus named on account of having bluish, or lead-coloured spots on either side of the nose, considered by some as resembling a butterfly's wings. The face is quite white. There is also a black butterfly smut. A good fancy rabbit must also have other marks. These are a blue or black patch of fur on the back called a saddle, with the tail the same colour as the snout and back. The legs are white and there ought to be dark strips on each side of the body in front, passing backwards to meet the saddle and uniting on top of the shoulders to form what is called the Chain, because it has the appearance of a chain or collar hanging round the neck! There was no attempt to standardise the markings until the National English Rabbit Club was formed in 1891.

The modern rabbit is well proportioned but not cobby, the weight is 6-8 lbs, the fur is dense and short and the body colour is white. Markings are in various colours: black, blue, tortoiseshell, grey and chocolate. The body markings are well defined in the Standard and carry 67 points out of the total 100 points.

ENGLISH SILVER

History shows that silver rabbits were in Britain at the beginning of the 17th century. This breed originated in Europe, probably France, yet the French give England as the country of origin. It was at one time known as the Riche (French for valuable). It was bred in its thousands in the London area. In around 1870 the skins were exported to Europe and fetched about £5 per dozen.The rabbit had other names and was known to the fur trade as Millers; Silver Sprig and Lincoln Silver were other names.

The present Silver bears little resemblance to the 19th-century rabbit. It appears in European Standards as the Argente Anglais in blue, fawn, cream, havana, brown and grey. It is of medium size, finely-boned with a short, glossy, fly-back coat and matures quickly. The body colours are evenly silvered all over. It is interesting to note that the Lincoln Silver was more of a fur-coated rabbit and that Lincoln was the centre of the hat industry. In the 18th and 19th centuries its fur was used in hat making. It took 40 skins to make one fur felt hat, and, even today, the top hat is a mixture of silk and rabbit fur.

FAUVE DE BOURGOGNE

This is a very well-known breed indeed, both as a show and meat rabbit. It originated in France from crossings of tawny-coloured wild rabbits and was created by A. Renard. It is a truly beautiful dual-purpose animal. Its weight is 3.5-5 kgs. It grows rapidly and is thickset and well muscled, with a rich tawny-red colour which is very even, intense and deep red, right down to the skin. The belly is paler, with the chin, undertail and eye circles also being much paler. This rabbit is found all over Europe and was re-created from crossings in South Africa in the 1970s. I think the Belgian Hare was one of the crossings.

OLD ENGLISH RED

The Old English Red is now extinct and no one seems to know anything about it nowadays. Perhaps some reader may enlighten me! I would be delighted.

FEE DE MARBOURG

The creater of this breed is unknown. It originated in Germany from Havana crossings; it is very well known in Eastern Europe. In type it is slightly thickset and well rounded, although it is finely boned in body. The head is short and sits firmly between the shoulders with no neck visible. The ears are strong and well furred and the colour is light grey-blue with a light brownish reflection which is more obvious on head and ears. The fur is very dense and silky and the eyes are bold and grey-blue in colour, with the ruby reflection (when viewed at certain angles) that is a sure sign of its Havana ancestry. The weight is 2.75 kg.

FLEMISH GIANT

Here we have two types. There is the original Flemish, and the English one, created by Christopher Wren (a distant relation of the famous architect Sir Christopher Wren). His daughter carried on working with the English Flemish and at the time of writing, 1999, she is 96. Both rabbits are crossings from Giant rabbits. The Flemish Giant is probably the best known rabbit in the world. It appears in practically every country where rabbits are domesticated and it has a long and very interesting history. Giant rabbits have been noted for centuries; there was an Italian Giant as early as 1555.

The Flemish Giant proper was bred on a very large scale in Ghent, where there were numerous amateur breeders, and they founded Flemish Giant breeding societies with odd names, such as Fearless, The Sunday Brothers, The Ghent Maid, The Young Shopkeepers, etc. This bears witness to the strong appeal this rabbit had. The societies were strong and active, and they even had their own particular pubs where the Giant breeders met, saw, spoke to, ate and drank only with other Giant breeders.

The original Standard was made in 1895. There are numerous copies of this Standard still around. There were two classes only – the Grey Agouti with a white belly and the Iron Grey with a dark belly; the latter became more popular in other countries. The German Giant Club was formed in Leipzig in 1897. From 1937 the Flemish Giant has been known as the German Giant. The French Standard was drawn up in 1919 and is much the same as the original Belgian one. Over time the heavy, clumsy rabbits were ousted by streamlined, lengthy rabbits. The craze for length was pushed to extremes and this gave the poor rabbit an unbalanced appearance which made it look as if it needed another pair of legs in the middle! It became known as the Folding Yardstick, Sea Serpent with a rabbit head, Greyhound Giant and Accordion Giant. German breeders very quickly bred a type with a more balanced body and all countries now aim for this type with a long cylindrical body, the whole being solid and firm. Ears are long, strong and erect with a length of 7-8 ins. The weight is 7-8.5 kgs. There are eight recognised colours in Belgian and French Standards but Holland has the most varied colours.

Flemish Giant: Double Champion 'Hampton Dark Steel' bred by Christopher Wren, pioneer breeder of the English Flemish Giant and the Chinchilla Giant.

The English Giant is one colour only, and much smaller at 11-12 lbs. The body is large, roomy and flat. The colour was dark steel grey, with even or wavy ticking all over the whole body except for belly and underside of the tail, which are white. This rabbit was exported to the USA in fairly large numbers. There is still a UK Flemish Giant Club with a very faithful following, although the numbers have decreased in recent years.

FLORIDA WHITE
This is a strong, compact, cobby rabbit with a weight of 5 lbs. It originated in the USA and its ancestors were crosses of Dutch, Polish and New Zealand White. The colour is pure white throughout, with bright pink eyes. The fur is of medium length and is of good texture and density. The coat is a fly-back variety, which means that if it is rubbed in the opposite direction the fur quickly returns to its original state.

AMERICAN FOX
This originated in the USA from crossings of Chinchilla, Self Checkers and English Silvers. The Checker is a large white rabbit with black ears and eye circles, black patches on the back side of the haunces and a butterfly smut on the nose. The creator was W. Garland. This Fox rabbit differs from European Fox rabbits and, in fact, it is the American Silver Marten that is the counterpart of the European Silver Fox. The American Silver Fox was admitted to the USA Standard in 1925 at the Colorado Springs Convention. The breeder was also a breeder of the American Checkered Giants and it is thought that he used self and other crosses. The colours are black and blue evenly silvered, its weight is 9-12 lbs and the fur resembles that of a real fox – fairly long with plenty of life and sheen. The coat should remain in an upright position when stroked from rump to head; it does not have a fly-back coat.

SILVER FOXES
These rabbits had their origins in England and Germany in around 1920. Their ancestry is Chinchilla crossed with Black and Tan. This beautiful rabbit goes under various names.

Germany	Weiss Grannen
France	Renard Argente
USA	Silver Marten
Holland	Zilvervos

It was originally bred to resemble the Canadian wild silver fox and is a modern creation with markings similar to the Black and Tan, although it is now bred in various colours. Blue followed the Black in 1920, and then came lilac and chocolate. It has also been dwarfed and rexed. The English Standard has been adopted in France. I actually took the first Silver Foxes to the International Agricultural Show in Paris during the 1960s – where I traded them for a pair of French rabbits which I think were Rhinelanders. In 1972, French official Standards admitted the English Silver Fox. The weight is 5.5-7 lbs; the chest, feet and flanks should be well and evenly ticked with silver-tipped guard hairs. Extended ticking up and over the back is to be considered as an added beauty.

SWISS FOX

I first saw this beautiful little rabbit in the 1960s at an International Show where two had been entered; I had never seen such a beautiful little rabbit. I was completely enchanted. Its ancestry is from crosses with the Angora, Chinchilla and Havana. It was created by M Teifer.

The Swiss Fox had nothing in common with the other Foxes or the American Marten. In 1926, M Teifer produced a Fox from crossing the Angora and the Chinchilla; a further crossing from brothers and sisters produced blacks with short coats and two Chinchilla does with long coats. He then crossed these two does with a Havana buck. In the first generation, the blacks bred well, the majority having long coats; these were used in further crossings and, in 1926, a Havana with a long coat appeared – the Fox for which Teifer had been searching. Among the youngsters he had long-haired blacks, whites and fawns. When they were shown in Germany, they caused great excitement and had great success, but then very quickly, and for no known reason, this lovely rabbit disappeared from Germany. The colour most bred is the Havana. The length of coat is most important and the minimum length is 4 cms.

GIANT BRITISH RABBIT

This was created by Mr Kirk from other Giants and the Flemish. It is a fairly rare breed and was first shown at the Alexandra Palace show in London in the 1960s. It is the largest of the British breeds and has a large roomy body, which is flat on top with a broad front and hindquarters, erect ears and bold eyes. The coat is very dense. Its colours are white, black, dark steel, brown and grey and its weight is not less than 11.5 lbs, but it must be over 16 lbs to gain points in the Standard.

GOLDEN GLAVCOT

The ancestors of this English breed are three brown rabbits: Siberian, Havana and Brown Beveren. It was extinct for many years until it was re-created by J. Irons and shown at Doncaster Show in 1976. Other breeders were scathing in their remarks, but I liked it, so he told me how to carry on the breed, which I did. I introduced a wild rabbit and, finally, made the wanted colour. It is now shown in Rare Breeds Classes.

The rabbit has a broad band of blue merging into brown that is tipped light red, and the whole is interspersed with dark brown. The fur is very soft, fine and dense and is shaped like that of the Beveren. There was also a silver and a blue Glavcot but these are now extinct, although I have heard that a breeder is trying to bring back the blue. The original name, Glavcot, has puzzled me greatly and I have not been able to learn its meaning.

GREY PEARL OF HAL

This is a lovely little rabbit which is Belgian-bred from the Havana and the Blue Beveren. It was created in 1910 by M Vervoort but is rare nowadays. The weight is 2 kgs and its size is in good proportion with its weight. It has a short, round head with short furred ears and its eyes are large, round and black – almost goggle-eyes. The fur is fine, dense, short and lustrous. The colour is an even pearl grey all over. It was originally called the Gouda.

HAM BLUE

This originated in 1900 and was bred by the rabbit club of Ham-sur-Heure. It was often mistaken for the Blue Flemish Giant, so a very strict limit was placed on its weight of 6 kgs. It did have some resemblance to the Flemish Giant but was not so long in the body and had a flat form. The head differs from the Flemish in that it is more oval in shape, instead of rectangular. The ears are shorter and not so wide, the fur is soft and lustrous, and of good length and the colour is slate-blue with no white hairs. This slate-blue is deeper than that of the Beveren, but not so deep as that of the Vienna Blue, which has tended to complicate things, especially with the Vienna Blue. This rabbit is no longer seen at shows and is practically extinct.

HARLEQUIN OR JAPANESE

This originated in France and its ancestry is that of the Dutch Tri-colour. It was first shown in 1887 in a class of 'common' rabbits and carried the name Japanese, although it was extremely different from the Modern Japanese or Harlequin. In 1887, it had three colours: orange, black and white. In 1895, M Rayson procured a pair from the Jardin D'Acclimatisation in Paris. They were imported into Jersey, Channel Islands, where they bred successfully.

In 1899, the French laid down a new ruling which excluded the white colour and named the colours yellow or orange with black. It did, however, have one oddity – a white nose which was eradicated by English breeding. The coat is very dense and silky and the length of fur is about one inch. Colours are divided into harlequins and magpies. There are two rex varieties: Normal and Astrex. Its weight is 6-8 lbs.

HAVANA

The name Havana pertains to the rabbit's very dark brown colour, not to its place of origin. The breed originated in Holland in 1898 and was said to be a chance mutation of common rabbits crossed with Himalayan. It had various names including Castor, Beaver Ingen and Fiery Eyes. It was introduced into the UK by Miss Illingworth in 1908. At that time there were two types of Havana – a large one weighing 4 kgs and a much smaller one weighing no more than 2-2.5 kgs. The differences between the two were negligible. Some breeders liked the small cobby type but the Dutch preferred the larger one; nowadays the small cobby one is preferred. There is also the French Havana which looks almost the same as the small one.

In 1902, the Dutch discovered yet another Havana, which was exhibited at Maastricht. It differed from the others in that it lacked the deep purplish sheen found in the coat. It was introduced into the USA in 1916 and the breeders there also bred the heavyweight Havana. The American breeders developed the Blue Havana created by Lee Owen Stamin. There is also a black. In the UK the original dark chocolate colour with the dark purplish sheen is the only colour recognised so far. It is interesting to note that many new breeds have Havana crossings.

It is a very compact 6-lb rabbit with a short neck and back and a very broad, rounded rump. The eye colour matches the coat but has a ruby glow when viewed from certain angles.

HIMALAYAN

The country of origin of this rabbit is purported to be China or North India, although European Standards say that its origin is Britain. It is supposedly found in

China in great numbers and is used in sacrifical offerings in the early part of the year, with prayers that the crops and fruits of the earth may increase and multiply like the 'black-nosed rabbit'. When first introduced into Britain it appeared in London Zoo. Its ancestry includes crosses using Silvered Rabbits.

A famous French breeder, M Schaedlter, who taught me all I know about European rabbits, once said of the Himalayan: "If it is not a good Christian it is not its fault for it has been well baptised; it has been known as Russian, Chinese, African, Egyptian, Lapin d'Anvers, Mock Ermine, Black Nosed Rabbit and the Windsor Rabbit." It is, however, an important little rabbit that has gone from country to country because of the great demand for its pelt (Mock Ermine). Europe had two sizes of the breed – large and small – and here they are known as the Russian Rabbit. The fur is short, fine and pure white, and the feet and legs are long and slender with black 'stockings'. The nose carries black oval markings well up between the eyes and the tail; other colours are blue, lilac and chocolate and the ears are black. The weight is 4.5 lbs. The eyes are bright pink.

THE LARGE HIMALAYAN OR RUSSE
This was created by Mlle Lemaire who used no crossings to achieve it. All its black points must be as black as possible and the eyes are ruby. This is altogether a strong, compact, well-muscled rabbit, which can be confused with the Californian.

HOODED RABBIT
I cannot resist including this variety, as its description is so unusual. As well as 'hooded', it was also known as the Muscovy or Moscow Rabbit. It appears in *Bewicks Quadrupeds* of 1791 and is described as having a double skin over its back into which it can withdraw its head, with its fore legs concealed likewise in a part which falls down under its throat. There are small holes in the loose skin on the back which admit light to the eyes. The body colour is cinereous (ash grey) with a brown head and ears. I was told that a manuscript of this animal, with a drawing by Mr G. Edwards, was preserved in the British Museum. On the off-chance that this might be true, I contacted the British Museum and, to my great astonishment, they confirmed the existence of the drawing and the account (above) given to the Royal Geographical Society.

HUSUMER
This originated in Germany from Dutch rabbits and was bred by H. Zeumer. It is a blue-eyed, white rabbit. It was also known as 'the patterned rabbit with blue eyes' because it existed long ago, with butterfly markings. Mr Zeumer, who was also a well-known judge, had to give up his rabbits and experiments on the outbreak of the Great War. The Husumer has now resurfaced and has a Standard, but it is still extremely rare. In the UK, for example, there is only one breeder.

LAND KANINCHEN
This originated in Germany from Giant Mottled rabbits. It resembles the Giant Butterfly, but without the butterfly smut. Its nose is all white and the weight is 10-12 lbs.

LILAC OR DUTCH GOUWENAAR

It is of note because its country of origin is the UK, Holland and Belgium. It was created by Miss Illingworth in England in 1913, by Professor Punnet in England in 1920, and by M Vervoot in Belgium in 1910. Three crossings produced the Lilac: Havana and Blue Beveren (Dutch); Havana and Blue Imperial (England); Havana and Beveren and Chocolate Dutch. This really lovely rabbit, when bred by Miss Illingworth, was known as the Essex Lavender and, later, as the Cambridge Blue. In Belgium a similar crossing of Havana and Blue Beveren produced the Gris Perle de Hal in 1910, making this the earliest record of the Lilac.

It is a cobby type with a very dense, silky fur, without a fly-back coat. The colour is an even pinky dove colour throughout, right to the skin. The Dutch breeders have the best colour – a true pinky lilac. The UK breed has lost this colour, and, probably, needs a new input of Havana colour.

GREY SWISS

This breed originated in Switzerland and was bred from blue rabbits and agoutis. Bred in 1920, it is a small, very cobby breed which has the characteristic of being alert and having a profile like a sheep. The colour is light grey-blue with plenty of guard hairs shaded at the tips. There are also isolated hairs with bluish pearly tips, giving the top a pepper and salt effect. The fur is dense with plenty of undercoat, with the top and guard hairs giving it a rich lustrous sheen.

LOPS

Any rabbit with ears that fall vertically is a Lop. This family has grown in the last few years. Now we have the English Lop, French Lop, German Lop, Mini Lop, Netherland Dwarf Lop, the Cashmere Lop, the Giant Cashmere Lop and the silvered Meissner Lop. The English Lop is the oldest and rarest of our fancy breeds. In fact, it is a wonder it has survived so long. It was mentioned in 1822 as being a lop-eared smut rabbit, having double or single smuts with black and tortoiseshell being the favourite colours. They were at the height of popularity in the mid-19th century and were exported to the USA and the Continent. It has been recorded that one breeder dispatched between 50 and 60 in one week! The ears were all-important and, when the ears did not lop properly (i.e. horn lop, oar lop, or half lop), the rabbit usually wore a little leather cap with two slits. The ears went through the slits from the underside and the two ends were tied under the rabbit's chin to keep the ears in their proper lopping place; this was the brainchild of an American breeder. The old Lop was a huge creature weighing up to 20 lbs, or even more.

In 1897, at the Brighton Show, the cup was won by a Lop of 17 lbs in weight with 21.5 ins ears. Between the wars it gradually decreased in popularity and, after 1945, became very rare indeed. As the passion for growing ears was the main object, the poor rabbit suffered. When I saw my first English Lop it was a poor thing indeed. It took me three years to buy a pair. Ultimately, I got a three-year-old doe and was offered a sterile buck which turned out to be not so sterile. I had my first litter from that pair. I noted that the body of the Lop had indeed been forgotten and I was determined to improve it. But how?

I read all the rabbit literature available, discovered that the French Lop was a cross from the English Lop and went to France and bought the Paris Show winner for £5! I took one youngster back and bred it with the English Lop and 10 years later, when

I showed it in Paris, it nearly caused a riot because I had crossed it back to the French Lop. The head judge asked me "What have you done to the English Lop? We have never seen such Lop". I told him that I had looked up the French Lop ancestry and discovered that the English Lop was an ancestor. He laughed and laughed, thinking that it was a huge joke and said "Now why didn't we think of that?". From there on, the Lop improved and was, from the 1960s onwards, a good rabbit behind the ears!

> *The English Lop finds itself in the meat rabbit category in hot countries because its ears provide a first-class cooling system – the fur is thinnest on the ears and the blood vessels are nearer the surface. For tropical production, it is crossed with the New Zealand White.*

A useful note to remember about lopping ears is that it has been proved that litters born in summer months tend to 'lop or flop'. This has been noticed in other breeds as well. The data for the rate of growth of lop ears in a first-rate specimen is as follows:

4 weeks	11 – 16 inches
6 weeks	11 – 20 inches
8 weeks	20 – 22 inches
10 weeks	22.5 – 24 inches
14 weeks	24 – 25 inches
16 weeks	25 – 26 inches

The most important thing to know about lop ears is how to measure them. A rigid wooden rule is absolutely necessary. With the rabbit facing you, place the ruler behind the ears and lie both the ears along the ruler's length. Hold the tip of one ear firmly by your thumb, stretch the ears gently along the ruler and read off. For the width of ear, which carries more points than that for length, find the widest part of the ear, lay it on the ruler and read off. At shows it is necessary to have the assistance of a steward. Any colour is permissible. A blue was first bred in 1922 by the Brothers Lumb.

There is, actually, a German stamp, dated 1926, of an English Lop owned by one of Europe's best international judges, Mr Joppich. So if you are a stamp collector, it is a real find, especially if you are also a Lop breeder!

French Lop
This was bred in France by M Cordonnier. It was created from the English Lop and giant French breeds. It was also known as the Rounanais Belier (meaning 'lop ear'), and Normand Belier, and has been in existence as the French Lop since 1852. In fact, rabbits with hanging ears have been in existence for centuries without attracting any interest whatsoever. The French Lop, or Belier, was bred mostly for meat, and exported to Germany in 1869 and Switzerland in 1899.

It has a massive, thickset body which is perfectly balanced. The head is very well developed, with a boldly arched crown (made from a strong ridge of cartilage) from which the ears hang, close to pronounced cheeks. This characteristic placing of the ears resembles a horseshoe shape, due to the convexity of the outer aspect of the ears. The length and width are in proportion to the size of the rabbit. The most common colour is the agouti, although all colours are permissible, including the butterfly pattern, the harlequin pattern and the black and tan Lop. The eyes are deep-set.

Mini Lop
Also known as the Dwarf Lop, this is a classic example of a gallon in a pint pot! It should resemble its Giant relation in every detail, but with an ideal weight of 4 lbs 4 ozs.

German Lop
This is the same type as the French Lop but the weight is 6-7 lbs.

Netherland Dwarf Lop
This is the newest and the smallest Lop, with a weight of 1.25 kgs. It has a very large following in the UK and it may, in fact, become the most popular. The creator was Mr De Cok, who made the observation that, if the weight drops below 1.25 kgs, the rabbit becomes deformed.

Meissner Lop
The Lop originated in Germany from crossing of Lops and silvered rabbits by Herr Beck. It is the loveliest of the Lop tribe because it is not so massive as the French Lop, but it resembles the English Lop in type. It has a distinct profile with ear-length of 38-42 cms.

American Fuzzy Lop
The American Fuzzy Lop is a small breed (not more than 3 lbs in weight) that resembles the Cashmere Lop in many ways. The fur is very dense and evenly silvered with length of fur 1-1.5 ins. The recognised colours are: black, blue, yellow, brown, havana. Many woolly Dwarf Lops were sold and exported to the USA from the exclusive store Harrods in London.

Cashmere Lop
Bred from woolly Dwarf Lops by Mrs L.A. Plant, they were christened 'Thistle Downs'. The coat is made of very fine wool and can now be one of a variety of colours; there is also a Giant variety. Any resemblance to an Angora will cause disqualification in showing.

LORRAINE RABBIT
There are two distinct breeds of this rabbit:

- German (Lotharinger Riesen). This is a very large rabbit; it is grey-blue in colour, with long ears of which one is usually lopping; there is also a Brown variety. It is very well known in Germany as an excellent dual-purpose rabbit. It is apparently a cross between a Flemish Giant and a French Lop and is not extinct.
- A cross between the Flemish Giant and the Butterfly breeds. It is known as the German Checker, or Rhenish Checker, and it is more like the English Spot without the butterfly smut. There is no Standard for this one. There is, however, a Dwarf one of Dutch origin, created by Mrs Berman Van Schelven.

Rabbit breeds

THE LYNX

This German rabbit was created by Herr Hoffmans in 1920 by a crossing from the Fee de Marbourg and the Black and Tan; there is also a French version of the Lynx. Strangely enough, the UK does not have the normal Lynx, but they do have a Dwarf Lynx, Satin Lynx, Polish Lynx and Rex Lynx. The normal Lynx is soon to appear in the UK.

The European Lynx is a wonderful colour with three different components: the top colour is pale silvery blue (no white), the between coat is russet, and the base colour is white. The coat should be not more than 1 cm in length. The combination creates a rosewood colour. The English Lynx colour is orange and silver with the same basal white. The eyes are grey-blue with red reflection and the fur is short, dense and silky. Guard hairs are barely visible. It is a very little-known breed.

NETHERLAND DWARF (EUROPEAN POLE)

This breed originated in Holland and is of British, Polish and Dutch ancestry. The creator is not known. The European Pole, the German Hermelin and the Netherland Dwarf are all the same rabbit. Europe gives the UK the credit for Dwarf rabbits but, in fact, the whole history is highly controversial.

In 1884, the British Pole was imported into Europe and crossings with Dutch rabbits gave it the cobby type. The German Pole, or Hermelin, was certainly a Dutch cross and was blue-eyed and larger than the red-eyed white. In 1948, the so-called Pole arrived in the UK and, to avoid confusion with the native Pole, it was re-christened 'Netherland Dwarf', for the UK already had a small dwarf rabbit called the Pole.

It is possible that the UK Pole was a warren breed, for it is known that 1 per cent of all wild rabbits are white. I have seen them and they resemble our little Pole in every detail. Delamer included it in his list of small tame rabbits in 1804.

In the USA, there was also confusion with the names: Netherland Dwarfs were crossed with Polish, and the actual Pole was dubbed a bad Netherland Dwarf. Now things have been straightened out and the English Pole in the USA rejoices in the name of Britannia Petite! These dwarf rabbits have gained great popularity as they are economical to keep – which nowadays matters a great deal.

They come in a great variety of colours, graded under self, agouti, patterned, tan patterned, shaded and other varieties. Most breeds have been dwarfed, satinised and rexed.

Three years ago, at an International French show, I judged Dwarfed Angoras, the first I had ever seen, just like little snowballs. The desired weight of Dwarfs is up to 2.5 lbs.

NEW ZEALAND WHITE

The country of origin of this breed is the USA, the creator was Joe Wojcik and its ancestry was Flemish Giants, Angoras and American Whites. It is a very well-known rabbit and is now found all over the world, particularly where commercial rabbit breeding is practised. It is a dual-purpose rabbit yielding excellent meat production.

There have been several strains bred in various parts of USA from various crosses, but that of Wojcik is the most notable. It was accepted into the American Standard Book in 1925 and it came into Britain some time later, appearing both on the show bench and in commercial farms. It is a quick-growing rabbit – a youngster can make 4 lbs live weight at 8 weeks old. The adult weights 9-12 lbs.

The New Zealand is a firm, solid rabbit with broad, full hindquarters. It has a fairly massive head with thick ears. The British Standard is roughly the same. Its fur is extremely dense, thick and coarse enough in guard hairs to offer resistance when stroked towards the head. It should not be too fine in texture, harsh or wiry, with a fine dense undercoat with heavier guard hairs. The colour is pure white with pink eyes. There was once a mutation which caused the coat to be all-over curly but the owner killed it off!

NEW ZEALAND RED
This is another USA breed which was originated in the early 1900s and was well known by 1915. It was created by crossing the Belgian Hare and Golden Fawn Rabbits, but the creator is not known. Its colour is a bright reddish sorrel that is not so dark as mahogany. This colour must go right down to the base of the hair. These rabbits are currently bred in South Africa.

BRITISH NEW ZEALAND RED
This is a golden red rabbit with lighter shading on its flanks and with hazel eyes. The fur is dense and harsh in texture and lies close to the body, with plenty of guard hairs. This is very different from the US Red, which is also 8 lbs heavier.

NEW ZEALAND BLACK
This was also bred in the USA and was developed by the crossing of a New Zealand White Buck and a Red Doe. It was bred first in California and there were several creators, the best known being Dr De Castro. It is the newest variety of the New Zealand and was bred first in 1949 from a New Zealand Red doe and a New Zealand White buck. Somewhere along the line the Giant Chinchilla was involved. It was first shown in the USA and accepted into the official Standard in 1958. There is also a British Black New Zealand and in the UK, in 1980, the first Blue New Zealand was shown, which was created by K. Brooks.

OPOSSUM
This is found in England, Switzerland and Germany and its ancestors include Silver Fox and Rex breeds. In Europe it was found accidentally when breeders attempted to imitate the fabulous silver Blue Fox. This gave rise to a number of long-haired varieties. The creators were T.I. Leaver (England), H. Reiler (Switzerland) and F. Joppich (Germany). The Opossums appeared in a litter in Germany in 1925. Herr Joppich opined that it was a Rexed Fox. In Britain, Tom Leaver also set out to breed the Opossum, at some time in the late thirties I believe, which was a good 10 years after they first appeared in Europe. Reiler did not continue to work on the breed. It is now practically extinct and there is only one breeder left in the UK – J. Wood of Scotland.

The Opossum has a small, compact body with a weight of 6-8 lbs. The fur is dense, lustrous and soft and is carried at right angles to the body without fall, so that the pelt has the same appearance viewed from any angle. The undercoat is about one inch in length and the whole coat is covered with fine white hairs of 1.5 ins long with a slight curl. The head, ears, feet and tail are not silvered.

PALOMINO

There are two types of Palomino – the Golden and the Lynx. This breed originated in the USA from a mixture of tawny and beige rabbits. It was first bred in 1952 by M. Young of Washington, and was originally known as the 'Washingtonian'. The rabbit was of a golden corn colour and, when suggestions for a better name came up, it became the 'Golden Palomino'. It is a very good commercial type of rabbit with meaty muscle on fine bones.

Mr Young says he bred sports (mongrels or mutations) from sports and began the breed solely from tawny and yellow-brown rabbits. He line-bred, out-bred and cross-bred. From this came beiges and from them came the golden shade. From this shade he came up with a fawn colour and from those rabbits came the Lynx Palomino. The weight is 9-10 lbs; the colour is gold with a cream undercoat and light gold guard hairs.

GIANT PAPILLON (FRENCH BUTTERFLY)

This is a French breed created from a marked (patterned) rabbit. The creator is not known. The breed, however, is very well known and can be found all over Europe and is always known by the country it is bred in, for example, in Germany, it is known as the Germany Butterfly. However, in Holland it becomes the Lotharinger and Switzerland calls it the Mottled Rabbit. It can truly be called a European, although it is also known in the USA and is called the Checker there.

In 1882, the writer Bonnington Mowbray mentioned the rabbits with two smuts – one each side of the nose, forming the butterfly smut. There was also one called the Egyptian Smut, 'Tanzac' or Japanese, but it was not quite the same as the modern one (the smut had originally consisted of two coloured patches, one on each side of the nose, but it has become like a butterfly with outspread wings and the nose is now coloured). In 1912, it was stated that all butterfly breeds came from a very old common rabbit. This rabbit was outstanding for having a very long stripe down the spine, a large coloured patch on the haunches, coloured ears and often a coloured smut on the face. Giant Papillons presented a challenge to keen breeders who were always on the lookout for something new. For example, there is the US Checkered Giant which stems from this tribe of smuts, patches and spots, and there is now a much smaller edition of the Dutch Lotharinger, weighing 2.2-3 kgs. The pattern, patches and smuts were originally black and these are still the most popular. Blues come a close second, followed by the chocolates.

SMOKE PEARL

This is one of the very, very few breeds created in Scotland from crossings of Sables. The creator was probably a Mr Stenhouse. It made its first appearance as the Smoke Beige and was known as this until 1932. It was bred in two colours. It is a small neat rabbit of 6-7 lbs. Its 1.5 ins-long fur is very dense and soft with the undercoat much more so; the colour is smoky-blue, shading to pearl light-grey on the flanks and belly.

PERLFEE

This little rabbit is a German breed created by Herr K. Hoffman by crossing the Havana and the Marbourg Fee. It is a very little-known variety.

Its fur is very dense, with plenty of guard hairs, which are tipped light grey and dark grey, which gives the fur its blue-grey pearly look and it is said to be an imitation of the Siberian squirrel. It has a brownish triangle at the nape of its neck, with the remainder a greyish-blue with three admissible shades: light, medium and dark. The medium colour is preferred by judges and breeders. Cobby in type, it is a fairly small rabbit (weight 5 lbs) and is finely boned. It is now in the rare breeds club of the UK.

PICARD OR GIANT NORMAND

This breed originated in France. The creator is unknown. The ancestors are Flemish Giants and common agouti rabbits (wild rabbits). It is a very ancient, but still fairly well-known breed found in Picardy, Normandy, Brittany and Central France.

It has a short, thickset body with powerful muscles and firm flesh. The ears are black laced (bordered with a narrow edging of black, like wild rabbits), the weight is 3.5-4 kgs and the colour is that of the agouti. The fur is very dense and short with almost invisible guard hairs.

POLISH

The Polish rabbit originated in England, possibly from Warren rabbit crosses (although it could be from a wild one because, as mentioned before, one per cent of all wild rabbits are white). It is the smallest of the UK breeds and very old; in around 1850, when the name 'Polish' was established, Delamer included it in his list of small tame rabbits as having 'white red eyes' (pale pink). It was by no means a favourite and was said to be sickly, not a good breeder, very timid and, in fact, a funny, puny rabbit. The weight was 3.5-4 lbs. The only thing it had in its favour then was its fur, which served as an ermine substitute.

Today, however, its ancestor is one of our finest fancy rabbits and has a great and devoted following. Although the British modern type is not yet recognised in Europe, it has been used to breed the European Pole and has found a place in the USA as the 'Britannia Petite'. Like the Netherland Dwarf, it comes in all colours and varieties and is very neat in type, being both compact and very sprightly. I quaked in my shoes when confronted with a table full of Poles! We needed a team of stewards to field them as they flew up in the air and over our heads – absolutely fascinating little beggars! Someone told me that on show days some breeders gave their exhibits a teaspoon of Vodka to encourage their sprightly ways. It is the judges who need the vodka!

The fur is short, fine and close to the body and the eyes are either dark blue or red. The modern weight is 2-2.5 lbs.

THE REXES

These originated in France from mutations of mostly common rabbits. However, Professor Kohler and A. Wiltzer had the honour of rescuing this now very well-known fur breed. The first specimens were a sickly lot with long nails, atrophied tails and a most peculiar form, and many of the does were sterile. President Wiltzer of France bought the first pair, which were then known as Castorex, or King of the Beavers. At the Paris Show in 1924, Professors Kohler and Litard proved that the Rex was indeed a mutation. In 1952, Professor Kohler bought three Castorex bucks which he crossed to white, black, fawn and Chinchilla rabbits, and in 1926 he was able to exhibit Ermine Rex, Black Rex and Chinchilla Rex. He published his method in *La Revue Via la Campagna* in May 1927. He mated does of all existing breeds to

Castorex bucks, thus passing on the hereditary characteristics of the Rex.

In 1929, Rexes were admitted to the French Standard, a similar mutation appeared in Germany, and the Rex was introduced into Britain in 1926. It was an ungainly, ugly rabbit that was bare on the neck nape and had oversized ears. One breeder was quoted as saying "Rex? They should be called Wrecks." Their unique fur was recognised, however, and today, no other country in the world can boast of better rexed rabbits. The British breeder is, I believe, first and foremost a stock breeder who knows how to improve his animals; perhaps it is due to the climate. I would not care to speculate, but rabbit breeders all over Europe agree with this. Anyway, in a fairly short time we saw the results of the breeders' work and the Rex was transformed into a very good, healthy rabbit with a heavily plushy, velvety coat with no guard hairs. The European Rex has a slightly longer, more open coat of about 1.5 ins long.

The Rexes are now subdivided.

1. Self Rexes – having same uniform colour.
2. Shaded Rexes – having a dark saddle shading off to lighter colour on the flanks.
3. Tan patterned.
4. Foxes – all fox colours.
5. Marten Sables – orange and seal martens. (The newest colour is bronze).
6. Agouti Castors, Chinchillas, Lynx, Cinnamon and Opals (which have the hairs banded in different colours).
7. Miscellaneous – Harlequin, Himalayan, Californian, Alaska (which may just be the Black Rex), Satin Astrex, Opossum, Dalmatian, Otter, Blanc de Hotot.

RHINELANDER

This breed originated in Germany and its ancestors included the English Butterfly and the Harlequin. The creator is not known. It is one of the very few tri-colour breeds and is a very striking rabbit and a great challenger to breeders. It is a thickset rabbit but it is well rounded, with fur that is dense, silky and not too long; the guard hairs must not be too apparent in order to preserve the neatness and the outline of the coloured patches. The body colour is pure white with black and yellow markings, each of which must be clearly defined and not run into one another.

The head pattern is important. The entirely coloured ears can be all black or be mottled. The face has a mottled, butterfly smut with a well-rounded body and wings spread regularly, extending under the lower jaw. The eye circles are regular with no breaks in the circle. The cheek spots are of one colour but all other markings are a mixture of two colours. In the body pattern there should be an unbroken saddle from the nape to tip of the tail and the width of the saddle or stripe should be three-quarters of an inch. Patches on the flanks must be regular, with six to eight spots on each side, which should be well separated and not too big. Two colours are a must for the saddle and flank patches. The Dalmatian Rex differs in pattern, having spots all over the body like the dog.

RHONE RABBIT

This is a fairly recent breed and a real nightmare for any breeder. It is a tri-coloured rabbit but there is now also a bi-coloured with a butterfly smut to be bred out. Colours are imposed on the white coat and markings are like that of the Harlequin, but with spots between the body stripes. The spots can be black on a yellow coat or blue or black on a white coat, which makes it a most striking rabbit indeed. Ears can be mottled or plain black. Despite its complications there is a Standard and one or two usually appear on the show bench, but in Europe only.

SABLE

This was bred to simulate real sable fur. It is brown in colour and appeared first in litters from imported Chinchillas from France. Thomas Leaver saw its possibilities and developed it.

There are two varieties of Sable – this is not two different rabbits, but the same rabbit bred with a new coat colour. The Siamese Sable is self-coloured, but has shading from a dark saddle area to a lighter colour on the flanks. The Marten Sable is similarly shaded with white ticking on the chest, flanks, rump and feet. Both Sable coats come in three shades – light, dark and medium; the Standard describes both as a "soft and gradual diffusion of brown shades".

Siamese sable. From the Whippell Collection, reproduced from Fur & Feather, 1929.

SABLE DE VOSGES

This originated in France and the creator was A. Fritsch. Ancestors are Sable, Sable Rex, Thuringer and Angora. It is a fairly new breed and a most striking one. M Fritsch, a retired schoolmaster of Barr in Alsace, was among the first breeders of Rex and coloured Rex rabbits. He often made crossings to fix the characteristics conforming to Mendel's Law. It was when he crossed the Sable Rex, Thuringer Sables and Angora that he obtained a light brown that was almost identical to Pastel Mink. He crossed again and after six years his new breed was stabilised. Fur specialists consider that the pelt is of great value as it closely resembles that of the 'Palomina' Mink. The breed was standardised in 1964. This weight is 2.5-3.5 kgs and the colour a light sandy brown. The extremities are deeper in colour and the fur very dense and lustrous.

MARTEN SABLE OR ZIBELINE

This breed originated in France and England and was created in France by M Fraineau. The English creator is not known; it is, in all probability, an import into England. Germany also claims to have created this breed. The ancestor to the Marten Sable/Zibeline was the Chinchilla and its sports (mutations). It was exhibited for the first time by M Fraineau at the Paris Show in 1914.

It arrived in England in an odd way, when litters of imported Chinchilla produced brown youngsters, and it was from these unwanted rabbits that T. Leaver and D. Irvine produced the English Sable in the 1920s. The French Sable was further crossed with a white Angora.

There are two distinct types – Marten and Siamese; the Marten has white ticking on the chest, flanks and rump and the latter has the points and colour of the Siamese cat. It is further divided into light spice, dark and medium. The newest colour is bronze.

SACHSEN GOLD OR KARLSBADER GOLDLOH

In Holland and Britain this rabbit is known as the Thrianta – a crossing of Havana, Tan and Madagascar coloured rabbits (i.e. sooty fawn colour). Its origins were in Germany and Holland and the creators were Herr Bennack (Germany) and Andrea te Assan (Holland). Its weight is 2.75 kgs with the body being short and thickset. The fur is very close, soft and lustrous and of terrific density. It is a most brilliant orangey-red rabbit and this covers the whole body, except for the belly and under the tail which are much lighter and of a yellowish tint. The first yellow rabbits were noted by Sir John Evelyn in his diary as seen in Brussels on 8 October 1641: "They were of a perfect yellow colour."

ST NICHOLAS BLUE

This beautiful rabbit has almost disappeared, but not quite; it would be a great pity if it did. It is a native breed of Wass in Belgium. The original rabbit was a magnificent creature of great size – 5 kgs. It was a light sky-blue colour with a white triangular blaze on the face, the point finishing between the eyes and the base encircling the lips. Some specimens had white feet which were later eliminated by the breeders. The body was very thickset with long ears, which were wide at the bases. The fur colour is the lightest of all the blue rabbits.

It was a great meat rabbit with a very-much-valued pelt. In 1926, three pelts fetched 35 Francs, which was a very reasonable price then. Unfortunately, in 1928, the Standard was revised with the white blaze deleted and an all-blue rabbit was created. This caused a real uproar and no end of confusion among breeders of other blue rabbits. The breed lost its particular blue, which was, in fact, mostly due to the albino factor of the white face-blaze. I have seen this particular all-blue St Nicholas in about 1996 at the International Rabbits, Pigeons and Poultry Show in Utrecht, Holland.

During many years of judging at home and abroad I have noted that male judges have a very different view of blue from lady judges. It is most marked when judging blue rabbits, as there are so many variations of the blue (45 in fact) where density and texture can make a lot of difference.

SALLANDER

This breed originated in the Netherlands and was created by D. Kuiper. It is a fairly new breed, created from crossings of a Thuringer yellow Chinchilla cross-bred with Marten Sable Dwarfs. It is a smallish breed with a short, broad head. The fur is fairly short with a dense, but very soft undercoat. The colour is light cinnamon with brownish tips of guard hairs giving the coat an all-over 'hazed' look. The ear and face-mask are a darker colour. Like the Chinchilla coat, it is composed of three colours: the base colour is white, then cinnamon, topped off with brown-black veiling; the belly is the same dark colour with a white undercoat.

SATIN

This breed originated in the USA. Its ancestry is from mutations of the Havana and the breed was discovered by Walter Huey of Indiana. This entirely new coat mutation was discovered in a litter of chocolate Havanas in the 1930s. When they were first shown in competition against normal Havanas this caused a great protest – so much so that the new mutation was officially recognised as a breed in its own right. This Satin factor has since been bred into a large number of other breeds so now we have Satin counterparts for most of our breeds. It has an exceptional lustre, texture and density of fur and it also makes an excellent meat rabbit.

In the early days following the Great War, it was noticed that the British Belgian Hare carried satinisation, particularly on its front feet. Hares carrying this factor were eliminated in Britain but it is more than possible that some stock exported to the USA carried the factor which is a recessive (see Glossary).

The first Satin rabbits arrived in the UK in 1947 and were mostly ivory in colour. In Europe, particularly Holland, the Satin was imported by Van Der Klink and is now fairly well spread. In the USA, the accepted weight is 10 lbs, in the UK it is 6-8 lbs. The rabbit is cobby in type with fur of exquisite satin texture and sheen, which is one-and-a-half inches in length; colours are many. Patterned rabbits have also been satinised. Satinisation of any breed can be done by mating normal to satin. The first generation will produce normals and the second generation will produce 75/25 per cent normals/satin. The smooth-coated satin Rex has hair of approximately half-an-inch in length with a fine satin texture and sheen. The coat is very dense with no guard hairs. With rough-coated varieties, the satin fur must carry a curl or wave evenly all over the body. Any colour or pattern is recognised by the British Rabbit Council Standard.

SIBERIANS

There are two distinct type of Siberian:

1. The original type from northern latitudes in Europe. This ancestry was Angora crossed with Himalayan. This breed was also known as the Moscow Rabbit (not to be confused with the Hooded Rabbit), and is now extinct. This is a great loss indeed for it seems to have been of outstanding beauty. It was, in appearance, an Angora with the black nose, ears, tail and legs of the Himalayan. It was usual to mate the best Angora to a Himalayan with the darkest points. It took four generations of pairing to procure the almost perfect specimen. It was a most valuable rabbit, but, for some reason, it became extinct (perhaps the Angora rabbit breeders had something to do with it). Its weight was 6-7 lbs, its fur was long, woolly and as dense as possible and the points (i.e. ears, nose, tails and feet) were covered with short black fur.

2. Modern Siberian. This one originated in England and resembles the original. The first Moderns were brown and bred in 1930 by C. Banfield, and also C. Pope. The Standard was adopted in 1933. The fur is of the roll-back variety or so-called 'blanket fur'. When turned in a reverse direction the fur gives a sheared appearance and must show as few guard hairs as possible. The black colour must go down as far as possible to an undercoat of pearly grey. The fur is extremely dense and of a lovely texture with a glossy sheen and a length of 1.5 ins. It is now bred in brown, lilac and blue as well as black. I used a brown one when creating the Golden Glavcot.

SILVER MARTEN (USA)
The ancestry of this breed is Chinchilla and Tans. It is really a throwback to early generations where the Black and Tan was introduced into Chinchilla make-up – in fact, the rabbit is a Black and Tan minus the yellow factor. Like the English Silver Fox it comes in four colours: black, blue, chocolate and sable. Black is most popular. The Standard and appearance are much the same as the English Fox, with the exception of the sable colour, which is really a dark sepia.

THE SITKA
This breed originated in England and its creator was Mrs Kerr. The ancestry is Blue Beveren, Angora and black rabbits. This breed was created in 1919 and originally called the Black Beveren, but the name was soon to be changed to Sitka. They were sold in considerable numbers in 1922, but without any guarantee, as the new breed was known to throw both Blues and Angoras. The Sitkas had white bellies, which were soon bred out in favour of a blue undercoat. The fur was very dense, soft, silky and lustrous, with a length of about 2.5 ins. It was one of our finest fur rabbits, but is now extinct.

THE SQUIRREL (BLUE CHINCHILLA)
This breed was the first to be created in Scotland, in 1930. In fact it originated in Scotland and Holland; its creator in Britain was Lawrie Stenhouse. Its ancestry is Chinchilla, Polish and Sable. It is a neat, cobby rabbit with blue eyes and a weight of 5.5-6.5 lbs. This breed in its normal form is now extinct, but it does still exist as a Netherland Dwarf and Satin. The fur is extremely dense, rich and lustrous and is of about 1.5 ins in length; there is no woolliness. The top colour is slate-grey interspersed with longer hairs of deeper slate, which are evenly distributed throughout. There is a grey eye circle. The Dutch Squirrel was created by D. Vogel of Apeldoorn by using crosses of Chinchilla and Silver Fox and Argente Bleu.

SWAN RABBIT
This now extinct breed was probably a mongrel derived from Giant Breeds, in particular the so-called Patagonia. It seems to have been indigenous to the Isle of Man. It was a very large, ugly rabbit of 16-20 lbs weight, brown-grey in colour with a large, roomy frame. The ears were only 2 ins long, with their hollow insides pointed to the front. It was, like the Patagonia, a useful meat and fur rabbit.

THRIANTA (SEE SACHSEN GOLD)
There is a Dutch breed of a tan rabbit instead of black, blue or chocolate; the colour

is a rich, bright, orange-red, exactly the same as the German Sachsen Gold. It appeared in the Dutch Standard in 1957.

THURINGER

This breed originated in the Province of Thuringe in Germany and was created by D. Gartner and E. Pieper in 1905 with crossings of the Himalayan, the Argente and Giant Rabbits. It is a very attractive rabbit – thickset and well rounded with fur resembling that of the Marten. The fur is very dense, short and lustrous and the weight is 4.25 kgs (show rabbits must conform to this weight). The colour is a yellow ochre or buff shade, with a sooty, veiled look on both sides of the body. Well extended on the rump are large, blue-black, sooty patches which should stand out well. The face-mask is deepest in colour, especially above the nostrils, and does not extend beyond eye level. The feet are sooty. It has now been introduced into the UK and actually improved by D. Medlock.

VIENNA

This breed originated in Austria in 1895, created by a J. Schultz, using grey-blue rabbits and silver Argentes. There was a large blue Beveren Rabbit in this ancestry as well as Blue French Lops. The Vienna was a large blue rabbit with quite a history. Belgian breeders of blue French or Belier Lops disagreed over the country of origin stating that it was a Belgian breed and not Austrian. Today's Standards state that it was Austrian. It is a very well-known breed all over Europe and it now begins to be popular in Britain. The weight is 4-5 kgs and it is of a thickset type with a cylindrical body that is very strong. The colour is very even and deep, dark, slate-blue with a warm tint; it is the same all over the body but is matt on the belly and under the tail. The eyes are grey-blue. It has been often said of the Blue Beveren that it was 'a salad of blue rabbits'.

The white Vienna was also created in Austria by Herr Mucke in 1907 from Dutch rabbits. This is also purported to be the Roubaisien rabbit, bred by M Pulinckx. It is a little smaller than the blue, but of the same type, with a very dense, silky, fine coat with long guard hairs, giving it great all-over brilliance. There is a very dense undercoat. The eyes are light pale-blue in colour.

GREY VIENNA

This is the same type as the blue Vienna with a very dense, tight fur. The top colour is even all over and bordered by a 3mm side black stripe under the top coat tips. The between colour should be a clear border of rust brown. The base colour is dark blue-grey. The colourings that are allowed are hare-grey, agouti and dark grey.

WACHTEBEKE RABBIT

This originated in Belgium from a rare colour crossing of the Brabacon and the Flemish Giants, and was created by M Pulinckx. It was a dual-purpose rabbit of meat and pelt, but is now extinct.

The head and ears are blackish and the black becomes more and more brown-grey towards the tail. It has white markings, an even, thin, white neck collar and white throat and white feet. It has never had an official Standard. It was bred mostly in North Flanders and was the principal meat source of the poorer populace. It was a very good mother and capable of managing large litters.

THE LION RABBIT

This rabbit appeared in a litter in France and in crossbred litters in Belgium. The breeders were attempting to produce a long-coated Dwarf. It has not yet been recognised as a breed in Europe, nor has it been Standardised there. It is a small rabbit; its weight is, apparently, about 3 lbs 8 ozs but there are reports that it is as small as 2 lbs. It has an excellent temperament. Unlike the other long-haired Dwarf, the Cashmere, it has a long-haired ruff around the neck and a certain amount of longer hair on the flanks. It is beginning to breed true and it comes in many colours, but the main one is creamy gold. There is now a British club for this little rabbit which can sit in the palm of your hand, or fit in your pocket! However, I know, from my own experience when I was attempting to recreate the Golden Glavcot, that it took thirteen years until that rabbit was recognised by the Rare Varieties Rabbit Club.

There is another new breed, that has not yet been seen, which is derived from the Castorex Ovator and is being bred in France in a small commercial stud. It is said to have a most wondrous fur, but no further details are available yet.

The creator of a new breed usually submits the Standard for the new rabbit to the governing body for acceptance into the Standards Book before being allowed to show the new breed. Also, the rabbits must have been breeding true to the original progenitor for at least four to five litters. The Rabbit Standards Book, usually revised every five years, is the rabbit breeder's bible.

Note: there is now an International Breeds Standard book, produced by the European Confederation of Rabbits, Pigeons and Poultry. It will be most useful in judging at European International Shows.

CHAPTER 12

EXHIBITING RABBITS

Who judges the exhibits? Is it the judge or is it the Standard? Exhibiting can be fun but it should be remembered that it can also be a bit of a battleground.

Sooner or later, the committed rabbit keeper will decide to show his or her rabbits. Rabbits cannot be exhibited at shows unless the breeder is a member of, or registered with, the country's governing body. In the UK, this is the British Rabbit Council (BRC). All countries in Europe have their own governing body and they are all run on the same lines. The world of rabbit shows can be quite baffling to a newcomer. The language is full of jargon and there is a healthy competitive spirit, make no mistake about that!

I shall never forget my first show. It caused no end of a joke, which I never lived down. I had only one rabbit so I bought one ring from the BRC. I did not know what to do with the ring so I tied it to my allotted pen. I did not know it was supposed to go on the rabbit's hind leg. After that howler, the Scottish Rabbit Club took me under its wing and my education into the rabbit fancy began and has never ended. I shall always be grateful to the British Breeders for putting up with me all these years.

In Europe and the USA rabbits are judged strictly to Standard with points being awarded according to what is laid down in the Standards (the maximum is a rarely-achieved 100 out of 100). Most countries have their own Standards of exhibiting and judging rabbits. There are now 21 countries in membership with the European Confederation of Rabbits, Pigeons and Poultry, with Russia and Japan being the latest applicants wishing to join the Confederation. For the last few years the EEC (Entente Européene de Cuniculture) committee has been compiling an International Standard for all countries and, in Europe, there is now an International Standard which allows judges to use the same points system from country to country for the same breed. The European Standard awards 20 points for type, 10 points for weight, 20 points for the condition of the fur, 15 points for the head, ears and eyes, 15 points for the top coat colour, 15 points for the undercoat colour and 5 points for the general condition. All breeds are graded as to weight and size.

1. JUDGING DIFFICULTIES

As you might imagine, until now it has been fairly difficult to be an international judge. Although there are Standards of rabbits, the same breeds often have different judging methods and even different names; for example the Himalayan is known in Europe as the Russe or Russian, and the Japanese was renamed in 1939 when War broke out, the British name becoming the Harlequin.

In the UK, rabbits are judged by comparison – one against the other: the best adult buck, best adult doe, best youngster (under four or five months old) buck and doe. Extra classes can be added, as an extra entry fee can help to offset the cost of setting up the show. Then, at the end of the day, all the Best of Breeds compete against one another for the coveted Best in Show. This is when the nail-biting begins! The best of each section is brought forward for assessment by a jury of judges, with a senior judge having the final word. In the USA, rosettes, ribbons and cards are given but no prize money is awarded.

The exhibition of rabbits in Europe generally takes place in autumn and winter only; spring and summer are the breeding periods. In the UK, however, there are shows all the year round – country shows, agricultural shows and specialist club shows, although the biggest shows are in autumn and winter when rabbit coats are at their very best.

2. RABBIT IDENTIFICATION

Each rabbit intended for showing must have an official identification, which in the UK, since 1926, has been a ring on a hind leg. Rabbits are rung at around eight weeks old, although some are rung earlier and some later, depending on the breed and the rate of growth. This is purely a means of identification which is difficult to remove once fitted. Rings are produced in varying diameters to suit the different breeds and bear the letters BRC, the year and a letter of the breed. The letters correspond to the breeds as shown on the next page.

3. DO'S AND DON'TS OF STEWARDING

This comes from the South African Rabbit Club.

- Don't make yourself so comfortable that the rabbit uses your chest for a pillow.
- Don't judge the exhibit. That is not your job.
- Don't pass any comments on the condition, shape, size, structure of the rabbit either to yourself or to a fellow steward.
- Don't be so interested in the other rabbits that the first reminder is a bite from a neighbouring exhibit.
- Don't strike or maul the rabbit in any way. No pinching or pulling out little bits of fur.

RABBIT IDENTIFICATION

(A) Polish

(B) Argente Creme, Dutch, Himalayan, Tan, Tri-Colour Dutch, Mini Rex

(C) Argente Bleu, Argente Brun, Dwarf Lop

(D) Chinchilla, Deilenaar, English, Havana, Beige, Lilac, Perlfee, Sable, Siberian, Silvers, Smoke Pearl, Thrianta, Cashmere Lop, Golden Glavcot, Squirrel, Foxes (except Swiss), Wheaten.

(E) Angora, Argente Champagne, Harlequin, New Zealand Red, All Rex, Satins, Swiss Fox, Sussex

(G) Belgian Hare, Beveren, Blanc de Hotot, Pointed Beveren

(H) Blanc de Bouscat, Blanc de Termond, Flemish, French Lop, English Lop, British Giant, Giant Papillon, Meissner Lop, New Zealand Black, New Zealand Blue, New Zealand White, Vienna Blue, Vienna White

(K) Miniature Lop

(L) Alaska, California, Chinchilla Giganta, Rhinelander, Thuringer, German Lops, Sallander

(X) Netherland Dwarf

- Don't throw or push your rabbit to the judge; he will prefer to take it from you.
- Don't hold the ears, or lift it by the ears or lift it by the fur on its back.
- Do wipe your hands before handling a white rabbit – also handle it lightly.
- Do take a rabbit from the next steward if he is struggling with more than one and yours is well behaved or has already been judged.
- Do treat your own rabbit exactly the same as another.

4. SHOW ETIQUETTE

This comes from the West Australian Club.

- Arrive at the show in time for your rabbits to be vetted.
- Have them penned before judging starts.
- Refrain from talking to other exhibitors at the judging table.
- Stand away from the judging table if you are not interested in the judge's remarks.
- Refrain from indicating which is your rabbit.
- Refrain from interfering or commenting on the judging; wait until the show is over.
- Please do ask if you can help. It will be much appreciated. Pens have to be cleaned. Pens have to be taken down, stacked and stored. All debris, straw, sawdust etc. has to be swept up and bagged. Too often exhibitors leave when the judging has ended and only the 'faithful few' are left to clear up after a very long and hard day. Think about it.

5. RINGING YOUR RABBIT

The easiest way is to have the rabbit on your lap with its head pointing to the side. Gently ease the ring over a hind leg. Push it down towards the hock and then carefully pull the leg straight out behind the rabbit – the hock joint will now straighten and the ring can be easily pushed over it. It is advisable to check the ring regularly, either to ensure that it is still on, or, the other extreme, not chafing the flesh. If the ring should become too tight, get it removed at once; jeweller's scissors are ideal.

Other methods of identification are tattooing and ear studs – the latter usually being carried out in commercial outfits. Ear studs are now being discarded because they have caused sore ears, torn ears, inflammation etc., and are also liable to catch on the handler's cuffs etc. Tattooing is a method used all over Europe.

6. SETTING UP A SHOW

Setting up a show entails a great deal of work for the host club. A show hall has to be booked, as do the judge, or judges if the show is a large one catering for all breeds. A show committee is appointed, with a manager and a show secretary who deals with all entries and sees to penning. Stewards are appointed to help in putting up the pens and numbering them.

The penning is important. Pens can be hired or borrowed from other clubs which are lucky enough to have their own. They must have solid floors, backs and sides; the fronts should be of strong wire, with doors which can easily be opened but which will remain securely fastened. There are also special factors to consider, such as the requirement for large rabbits to have larger pens and the Angoras' need for a special tray to fit inside the pen to keep the Angora coat clear of the pen floor.

Each exhibitor is given an entry card which has the allotted pen number on it. In very large shows the feeding and watering of exhibits is carried out by the night stewards, and bedding is also provided unless the exhibitor decides to supply his own. Once the rabbit has been vetted it must not be removed from its pen unless by order of the show manager. Any sign of ill health in an exhibit is reported to the show committee; the sick rabbit is then removed to its own travelling box and the owner is notified.

The judges and stewards are usually volunteers. They fetch and carry the rabbits from pens to the judging table and return them. The book steward is either appointed by the committee or, very often, a married judge has his or her spouse to keep the judging book. The book steward checks all rabbits, and a sticker with the pen number is stuck on the rabbit's ears. She or he has the judge's book of entries of which rabbits have already been entered in the appropriate classes, then notes the judge's placing of exhibits and ensures that rabbits are returned to their pens after judging. Main rabbit shows are always held in winter when coats are at their best.

7. THE JUDGE

The judge is all-important and must have a sound knowledge of the breeds and the rules and regulations as laid down by the governing body. However, most judges carry the Breed Standards, plus the rules and regulations book, in their pockets, along with a pencil and a ruler. It is also wise to add a few sticky plasters for bites and bad scratches.

The Rules and Regulations book can be a proper nightmare. Rules, amendments, amendments to amendments. They can be endless. Many a time I have wished Moses had written it. Ten Rules would be ideal!

In the USA and the UK and, indeed, all over Europe, the judge must have bred

FAULTS IN TYPE

Camel-backed.

Hollow-backed.

Chopped-off rump.

rabbits for four consecutive years. In Europe, in fact, the system is tougher. You must apply to be a trainee judge, sit an exam and do practical judging, possibly of ten breeds at a time, under a senior judge at important shows. It takes some time to be fully accredited. In the USA, an applicant must have an endorsement (a written reference) from at least two registered judges and an applicant for a judge's licence must have taken part in a judges' conference.

The judge must be honest and definitely impartial in judging and must not allow breeders who steward their own rabbits to embarrass him or her. Stewards should never try to influence the judge, of course, but most judges recognise this type of behaviour and have their own ways of dealing with the problem.

As well as the all rounder judge (one who can judge any breed or all breeds), each specialist Breed Club has its own panel of club judges. The Breed Clubs are a great get-together affair, with everyone showing the same breed. There is much talking, and arguing is the order of the day! It is here that the judge comes in for a good deal of criticism and showmanship can run riot if the judge does not keep an eye on it. It is considered to be in bad taste, and an offence, to try to influence the judge in any way with regard to the ownership of an exhibit. The best thing for an exhibitor to do is to remember that the entry fee pays for the judge's opinion, and that the choice made is final!

The same ruling applies to grooming the exhibit as soon as it arrives on the table. All grooming and training of the exhibit to pose should be done at home before the exhibit arrives at the show. If this is carried out properly, then all that is required at the show will be a quick smooth of the coat with the hands – with no spitting on hands either!

THE DEWLAP

Single regular dewlap.

Irregular dewlap.

Double dewlap.

Excessive double dewlap.

LEG FAULTS

Bow-legged.   *Knock-kneed.*   *Flat-footed.*

A well-known American judge has pointed out the great difference between UK and US judging. He stated that: "in America, we judge mainly on conformation or balanced body type, firm flesh, smooth hips. In Britain, most breeders are very strict about fur and colours and for the most part this is about 40 per cent better than ours." However, conformation should always be the first quality considered in any animal, for without type you have nothing; I personally believe that the American Standards, with the emphasis on type rather than the British preoccupation with colour, are preferable. Even our farmers today are now waking up to the loss of type in our native breeds, following the influx of foreign breeds after the last war, when some horrendous mistakes were made.

The American judging system has now arrived in the UK and I have noted that some club shows have a visiting American judge. At American shows, the exhibits are brought to the show with their own cages and each is judged thoroughly by keen inspection and comparison. After the judging is over, the judge is available for answering questions and for giving his reasons for his particular placing of the rabbits. This is a system I heartily agree with; too many judges 'hop it' as soon as their last rabbit is placed. The list of Registrars is held by the American Rabbit Breeders Association (ARBA) and they are responsible for the registration of pure-bred rabbits. The registration number, if tattooed, is marked on to the rabbit's right ear and the breeders' mark is put on the left ear.

All Rabbit governing bodies produce their own Standards of Perfection. These contain weights (minimum, maximum and ideal), points on conformation, colour markings on coats (Fur, Rex, Satin, Angora), slight faults, grave faults, and disqualifications. In the UK, Standards are reviewed every five years.

Now I will put my head on the block. If you ask any lady breeder why she chose a particular breed, inevitably the answer will be: "I fell in love with it." This love is not so evident in the male. Just watch a lady judge crooning soft words and sweet nothings to a table full of rabbits and see how tenderly she handles them, with a caress in every touch; now look at the male judge and his rabbits – up and down the table he goes as the rabbits are seized, bounced and chucked into place. No love affair here – no wonder they get bitten and scratched!

EAR FAULTS

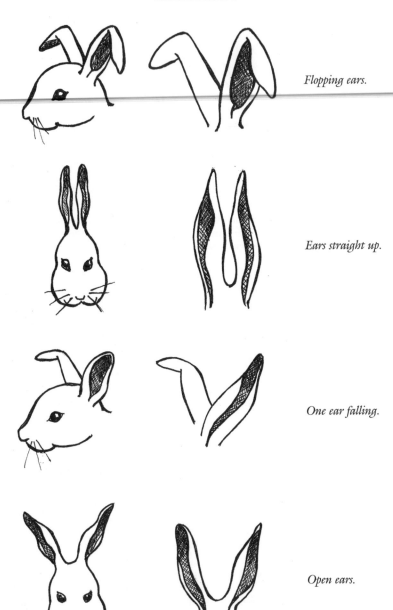

Flopping ears.

Ears straight up.

One ear falling.

Open ears.

TAIL FAULTS

Trailing tail

Tail held on one side.

Screw tail.

It also surprises me that invariably male judges cannot agree when it comes to judging coloured coats. Colours to most of them present a problem, particularly with blue. You will not catch the lady giving the rabbit 'the chop!' if his colour is off-key, his spots are in the wrong place, his saddle is broken or his tail skewed; she is more likely to kill a rabbit with kindness.

My first judging was at Peebles Agricultural Show. Peebles is a small town on the banks of the famous River Tweed, in Scotland. The Rabbit show was held in a tent right on the bank. When I started judging the 'old boys' ganged up – their idea of fun was to criticise everything I did; how my knees shook! At last, I made my final choice and one old breeder burst out "Look what she's done, God Almighty! – lads let's throw her in the Tweed.". I literally took to my heels and fled straight into the beer tent, where they found me and revived me with a stiff whisky.

8. PET RABBIT SHOWS

For judging at pet rabbit shows at schools or elsewhere, cards are usually awarded with rosettes for the best boy's and the best girl's rabbit. It is best remembered that one is not judging pedigree rabbits. The main prizes are for health, condition and cleanliness. I always enjoy this type of show and make a point of having a stock of 'Commended' cards so that no child goes home disappointed. On the back of each card I write a note of how well behaved, well fed or well groomed the rabbit is, if it looks as if it has its share of tender loving care. I have found that this prevents a lot of heartache among young exhibitors. From this type of show many children progress to pedigree rabbits and in no time get hooked on their hobby.

9. IMPORTING RABBITS

Sooner or later, the serious breeder will think of importing rabbits, either to have a new breed improved, or to improve an existing breed, or just to be

159

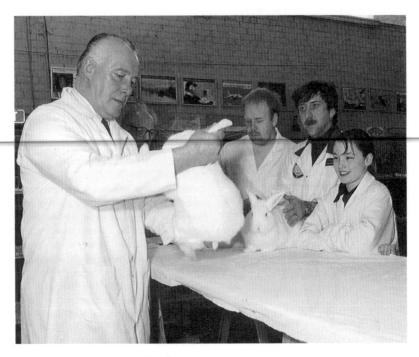

The judge must have a thorough knowledge of each breed standard.

able to say "I am the only one with this breed in the country". All are laudable sentiments as they will help to keep a fresh interest in the rabbit world, as well as bringing much wanted new strains into the country.

I would not buy or import a breed without seeing how the owner manages the rabbitry, and inspecting the rabbits in their home environment. The rabbits will not cost any more than if you were buying them unseen. Even buying through a go-between is not very satisfactory unless you are entirely sure of his or her credentials. I have attended many international shows and have seen prices paid for the not-so-good stock, and then I am shocked at the prices asked by the buyer when he arrives back in his own country.

It is important to know all about the breed. US breeders, for example, got into a tangle over the British Pole and the Netherland Pole. Both Poles were completely different animals, with the British Pole having been around for a century, while the Netherland pole did not appear until 1948. The British Pole is now known as Britannia Petite. So do be careful!.

10. JUDGING LOPS

The breeding of Lops is such a strange and specialist story that it merits a section to itself. The lop-eared rabbit is first mentioned by Mowbry in 1822 and they became all the rage in London during the latter half of the 19th century. No rabbit was eligible for showing unless it was registered within a few hours of its birth and most were not considered to be Lop show rabbits unless they had ears at least eighteen inches long (the limit at Woolwich Show was nineteen inches). Eight months was the youngest age that they could be shown in most of the Metropolitan Shows. Entrance fees to the shows were either one shilling or one shilling and sixpence (perhaps the extra sixpence was for a better view). The Woolwich Rabbit Club held two meetings each month with a fee charged at each meeting of between five and nine pence. Most of the Societies offered prizes for Lops: three prizes for ear length, six prizes for the best black and white, blue and white, sooty yellow and white, tortoiseshell and self. There were also one or two prizes for weight. The Woolwich Club also offered a class for width of ear.

The rabbits were judged by the Society's members, of which there were generally five. When one of the judge's Lops appeared on the table to be judged, that judge retired 'out of consideration for the others'. After the judging, the rabbits were turned loose on the table for the benefit of visitors, who passed their criticisms as the rabbits moved around.

There were many complaints about ill-treatment. Outdoor shows were objected to because Lops, at the time, were kept in very warm rabbitries, so when they were sent to the outdoor shows they shivered all the time which caused the fur to look rough and staring. Snuffles and lung diseases occurred and these conditions were, of course, even worse on cold, wet and windy days. Pens were drenched with rain and the poor animal arrived back at home soaking wet in its box or hamper.

Also, show secretaries who took care of the entries unwittingly added to the rabbits' misery. Each breeder had to list, 'Food to be given, oats, green feed or milk and water. Just add yes or no and fix to your pen'. Unfortunately, many of these cards were green – arsenical green – and many a rabbit was poisoned by chewing the corners of the cards!

> *The following note gives a good idea of how the Lops were raised. A Lop breeder of the old school believed in heat in order to grow long ears! He kept 50 Lops in a small hut, which was 12 ft x 4 ft and 5 ft in height. It had no ventilation and was heated with paraffin lamps. The rabbits produced were very small but very long in the ear!*

An all-England Show was held at Walworth in 1879 with 18 classes and 72 prizes of cups and specials. There were 241 entries and Lops alone had 16 classes for self colours, brokens and greys. Other classes are interesting:

Two classes of Dutch, Black and White, Blue and White.
Angoras – 12
Belgian Hares – 24
Himalayans – 19
Silver Fawns – 7
Litter class
Other varieties
2 selling classes
1 class for weight. 1 cup for the heaviest.
1 class for thoroughbreds
1 class for mongrels which may be castrated.

Selling classes:
1 Lops – not to exceed 30/- (shillings).
2 To exceed 30/- but not to exceed 60/-

Sixty shillings was quite a price over a century ago, but there was money to be made, exemplified by the fact that many of these types of rabbit had been exported to the USA in large numbers since the 1850s.

Ears were all-important, as they still are today, but some extremely cruel methods were used to create the required lopped ear. A length of 18 inches was considered perfect but, in 1870, there was the odd Lop with 23-inch ears and, of course, considerable heat had been used, and kept constant, as the important thing to the rabbit keeper was to have uniform heat. The rabbits were kept in bakehouses and also kept in boxes packed around with urine-sodden sawdust. This also made the cleaning out of hutches an occasional job as the rabbits were usually vicious, and no wonder!

There was also another trick to improve the ear length and that was particularly cruel. The young Lops were taken close to a roaring fire and, after the ears were well heated, the breeder took an ear in each hand, giving three to four sharp tugs, keeping up a constant pressure. All the fine blood vessels of the ears were liable to be broken, so the operation was constantly repeated. Varicosed ears were commonplace.

Another practice was carried out in order to achieve a 'graceful fall of ears'. A little leather cap, invented in America, was placed on the rabbit's head and tied under the chin. Some caps had weights attached. Thankfully, today we have cruelty laws.

The rage for Lops was an intense one – this rabbit became known as the 'King of the Fancy'. Since the beginning of this century the Lop has undergone many ups and downs. When I started with Lops, the National Lop Club had only 33 members. It took me three years to buy a fertile doe – and it cost me a whole month's salary too!

As described in Chapter Ten, I thought the English lop was a poor thing overall and needed something done. At the time I happened to be reading *Caractères Sportifs des Principales Races de Lapins* by E. Mesley (1908-1910) and I discovered that the French Lop was a cross from the English Lop in the late 1850s. I decided to go back to that crossing and so I went to France to one of their big shows and bought a beautiful French Lop doe – a Gold Medal Champion - for £5. Her progeny were great and, after four years breeding, I put a youngster on show. It had a firmly muscled body, its ears were thick and firm and it stood on its feet, rather than lying, as Lops usually do, like seals.

As far as I remember it had ears that were 25 x 5.5-inch ears, and I went on to breed a rabbit with 27-inch ears. I gave some of the rabbits that I bred to other breeders to carry on the type, because for me that was all-important. It is pertinent to remember that Darwin, who had done a lot of research on the skeleton of the Lop, described it as a deformed rabbit. The skull bones and also the vertebrae were displaced. It consequently had an awful sharp and curved spine, which today is no longer evident. The ARBA now give 35 points for the body alone.

However, as I have said in the previous chapter, the ears do remain very important in the breeding of the English Lop and it is very important to know how to measure them. A rigid wooden rule is necessary. With the Lop facing you, place the ruler behind the ears and lie the ears along the ruler tip. Holding the tip of one ear firmly by your thumb, stretch ears gently along the ruler and read off. For width, find the widest part of the ear, lie the ear on the ruler and read off. When judging Lops it is necessary to have the assistance of a steward.

As mentioned earlier, the rate of growth of ears in the young is as follows:

4 weeks	11 – 16-19 ins
6 weeks	11 – 20 ins
8 weeks	20 – 22 ins
10 weeks	22.5 – 24 ins
14 weeks	24 – 25 ins
16 weeks	25 – 26 ins

NOTE: Youngsters born in June, July and August in the UK have a quicker rate of growth due to warmer weather.

There are two old newspaper pictures in my possession of two Lop winners at Crystal Palace Show in 1853, published by the *London News*. The accompanying paragraph read as follows: "The rabbits are three fine prize winners for weight and length of ears. The one in the centre belonged to Mr Hades. On the right, Mr Stinton's and on the left Mr W. Crick's." The prize for each rabbit was two guineas; changed days indeed! In 1963 at Perth Show I won 3rd and got 75 per cent of the prize money – two-and-a-half pence in old money!

For those who are stamp collectors, there is a most beautiful old German stamp of a very famous English Lop, owned by an equally famous international Rabbit judge, Herr Joppich. The rabbit was shown at an International show in Leipzig in 1926. For years Herr Joppich was cut off from shows and his friends when the Iron Curtain came down. He died just after it was lifted.

APPENDIX I

A-Z OF COMMON WORDS AND EXPRESSIONS USED IN THE RABBIT WORLD

Adult: A rabbit of breeding age, or above the age stated for young classes.

Adult coat: Usually produced for the first time when rabbit is between 6 and 9 months old.

Advisers: Appointed by the BRC (British Rabbit Council) to represent the council and assist rabbit owners with queries and problems. They can be approached for practical advice on breeding, exhibiting, feeding, housing etc. Letters to the council are passed on to the writer's nearest adviser. Each English county has between one and four advisers, depending on the number of registered breeders. Scotland has three advisers and Northern Ireland has one. Each adviser submits a yearly report to the council. At present the system is being reviewed.

Affiliated club: A Club which, on payment of an annual fee, is affiliated to the BRC (British Rabbit Council). This secures benefits for the club and its members.

Agouti: A coat pattern found in wild rabbits, Chinchillas, etc. The belly colour is white, the top coat has black tips with bands of yellow or white below, and the black decreases in intensity at the base to slate blue. The whole coat is interspersed with longer guard hairs which are black throughout their length.

Albino: A pink-eyed white rabbit. Because they are recessive to colour they will always breed true when mated together, but they may genetically carry the factor for any colour or marking which is masked by a double dose of albinism. Thus, when crossed with coloured animals some surprising results often appear.

Allelomorph: One of a pair of alternative characters of inheritance: e.g. black and blue, Angora and short hair, Rex and normal fur, Albino and colour.

All rounder: Applied to persons who are recognised as experts on all varieties of rabbit, as opposed to specialists, who are experts in a particular breed or a limited number of breeds.

Area club: A club, the activities of which are confined to one geographical area.

Ash colour: Faded shades of colour, found in some Rexes and Beverns.

Astringent: A property of some plants useful in scours in that it opposes any laxative effect.

Baby coat: The early coat of a rabbit, up to about three to five months.

Bagginess: Excessive fat or looseness of the pelt, often due to malnutrition.

Balance: Applied to type of conformation and means a good, pleasing type, in shape or conformation. It can vary from breed to breed.

Barred feet: Lighter strips on coloured feet, a common show fault in Chinchillas and Foxes.

Barrel-length: A long rounded body that is almost cylindrical (for example, the Flemish Giant).

Barrenness: The inability of a doe to bear young, infertility.

Base colour: Colour next to the skin.

Bare spots: Parts denuded of fur, particularly found on hocks of Rex breeds.

Blaze: The white markings running up the nose and between the eyes, as in the Dutch breeds.

Bloat or blown: Pot-bellied. A blown-up condition of stomach and intestines.

Bowed legs: Applied to fore legs bent or curved outwardly in the middle.

Breeder: The owner of the mother of a rabbit at the time of its birth.

Breeder's class: A class confined to exhibits bred by the exhibitor.

Brindling: Coloured or white hairs interspersed in the desired colour. Brindling is a common fault on the noses of some breeds.

Broken coat: Areas where the coat is affected by moult that expose the undercoat.
Brood doe: A doe suitable for breeding.

Buck: A male rabbit

Butterfly: The coloured mark on the nose of an English Butterfly rabbit, which resembles a butterfly with open wings. This is also found in Checkered Giants, Rhinelanders, more 'brokenly' in Lops and more faint in Champagne and Creme Argentes.

Carriage: The way and style in which a rabbit bears itself.

Castration: Removal of the male organs of reproduction.

Chain: The spots on the sides of an English rabbit running from neck to loin.

Charlie: Lightly marked English.

Cheeks: Rounded coloured areas on the side of the head of the Dutch rabbit.

Cheek spots: A single spot at the side of the eye in English rabbits.

Chest: The front of the rabbit between the fore legs and neck.

Chinchillation: The elimination of yellow from the coat, as in the Chinchilla. The agouti or wild colour is the opposite.

Chopped: Applied to type. Having the rump cut off abruptly, and falling vertically to the tail instead of being rounded.

Clean cut: The line of demarcation between markings.

Cobby: Stout and stocky.

Collar: The white area in the Dutch, now known as the saddle.

Common: Wild or warren-bred.

Condition: The physical state of the rabbit in reference to health.

Cowhocks: Hocks that bend inward causing the foot to turn outwards.

Crest: The tuft of wool or fringe on the forehead of an Angora which, with the tufts on ears and feet, provide the 'furnishings'.

Crossbreeding: Producing a rabbit (a 'crossbreed') by crossing different pure-breds or by cross-breds mated together.

Cyanosis: Lividness of the skin owing to the circulation of imperfectly oxygenated blood; blue jaundice.

Definition: In Chinchillas, the clear line of demarcation between the pearling and the undercolour.

Density: The number of hairs to a square inch on the skin. A specified density of coat is essential in all fur breeds

Dewlap: A pouch of loose skin under the neck, usually found on does.

Dual purpose: Generally applied to fur breeds which are useful for pelts and meat.

Ear label: Small gummed label bearing the pen number, which is stuck between the ears, or inside the ear, at shows.

Ear lacing: A black line of fur outlining the ear sides and tips in certain breeds.

Eye circle: The circle of fur next to the eye. It is coloured in the English and is found also in agouti and tan-patterned rabbits.

Eye stain: Circle of colour around the eyes in Himalayans, a common fault.

Fancy: The Rabbit Fancy generally embraces rabbit breeders who are mainly exhibitors. The Oxford English Dictionary definition is: 'The art or practice of breeding animals so as to develop particular points; also, one of these points.' The term 'fancy' or 'fancier' can, of course, apply to other types of fancy such as the pigeon fanciers and poultry fanciers.

Factor: The term used for hereditary characteristics. It is controlled by the genes in the chromosome.

Flop eared: An ear partially falling to the ground. Not erect.

Fly-back: The coat, when stroked the wrong way, easily flies back to its original position.

Foot stops: The white on the hind feet of the Dutch rabbit.

Fore feet: Front feet.

Foster mother: A doe used in the rearing of another doe's litter.

Front: The wool on the chest of an Angora.

Frosty nose: Sprinkling of light hair found on the nose of some tan patterned breeds, e.g. Foxes. It is a fault.

Full coat: Adult coat free from moult.

Fur: The undercoat next to the skin which is fine, soft and thickly interspersed with heavier and thicker guard hairs. The guard hairs should be visible down to the skin and extend above the under-fur to give body and density to the coat. It forms a protective surface for the under-fur (or base fur) and should be carried down the sides of the rabbit (the stomach fur will be shorter but dense). Note that woolly fur lacks the strong guard hairs.

Albinism is a recessive gene giving a white coat with pink or red eyes.

Dominant: *(of a gene) Producing the same phenotype in the organism whether its allele is identical or dissimilar.*
A white coat with blue eyes is the result of a dominant gene.
Recessive genes are usually masked by dominant genes.

Phenotype: *The physical constitution of an organism as determined by the interaction of its genetic constitution and the environment.*

Allele: *Any of two or more genes that are responsible for alternative characteristics, such as smooth or wrinkled seeds in peas.*

Gestation: The period of pregnancy. Usually 30 days.

Ghost: A very light Chinchilla with wide pearly band and little or no undercolour.

Guard hairs: The longer and stronger hairs found in the coat. These are absent in Rex varieties.

Herring bone: The saddle running down the back of an English resembling the backbone of a herring.

Inbreeding: The mating together of very close relations such as father to daughter, mother to son, brother to sister.

In kindle: A pregnant doe.

Intermediate: The coat prior to the full adult coat, which generally appears at about four to five-and-a-half months of age.

Kindling: The birth of a litter.

Lactating: The production of milk by the doe.

Line breeding: The mating together of rabbits of same strain, but not so close as that of inbreeding: e.g. cousins, aunt to nephew, uncle to niece etc.

Litter: The youngsters born from a single pregnancy.

Lop ear: Ears falling vertically.

Marked: patterned.

Mask: The mealy coloured shading on the face of a rabbit – a shade of brown that gives an almost speckled appearance.

Mendel's Laws: The principles of heredity, proposed by Abbot Gregor Mendel (1822-1884) who was originally a botanist. The Law of Segregation states that each hereditary character is determined by a pair of units in the reproductive cells: the pairs separate during meiosis so that each gamete carries only one unit of each pair. The Law of Independent Assortment states that the separation of the units of each pair is not influenced by that of any other pair.

Moult: The casting of one coat and the growth of new fur.

Mutation: The sudden origin of an entirely new type such as the Furs Rex.

Muzzle: The lower part of the face and nose.

Open coat: Loose coat.

Outbred: A mating of unrelated rabbits or lines in the same breed. This is used to upgrade a line within the same breed.

Outcrossing: Breeding unrelated rabbits or lines within the same breed.

Ovary: The female organ of reproduction.

Ovum: The reproductive cell produced by the ovary.

Pearling: The lighter band of colour in the Chinchilla coat which comes next to the undercolour.

Pea spots: Two spots at the root of the ears in tan pattern varieties when viewed from the front.

Points: 1. The ears, tail, nose, below the hocks and joints of fore legs in Himalayans, etc.
2. A scale of points in the Standards showing the ideal to be aimed for in different breeds (see Standards below).

Pot belly: Enlarged stomach due to fermentation of food causing the formation of gases. This is usually due to faulty feeding.

Pseudo pregnancy: A doe exhibiting all the signs of pregnancy but producing no young.

Putty nose: White spot on the nose extremity.

Roll back coat: A gradual return to the normal position of the fur when stroked from rump to shoulder. This is usually the case with short, dense coats.

Appendix I

Saddle: The area of white before the rump in Dutch.

Scours: Diarrhoea.

Screw tail: Tail twisted to one side.

Scut: A tail.

Season: The period when a doe will accept the buck. It is noticeable by a deepening in colour and swelling of the vulva. The doe may also be seen carrying bedding.

Self: A lack of pattern in the coat, the rabbit being the same colour all over. The undercoat is usually paler. Siamese Sables and Tortoiseshells are self, but they do show shading.

Shadings: Variation in shades from darker on the saddle to lighter on the sides.

Sheen: Lustrous effect with a brilliance of coat when in peak condition.

Silvering: A mixture in the coat of white guard hairs as desired in Silver varieties, but a fault in most of the other breeds.

Slate: The bottom colour in Agouti and Chinchilla.

Smellers: The whiskers.

Smut: The butterfly pattern on the nose.

Snipey: Narrow, elongated head. Rat-faced.

Speck eye: Small white specks in the iris of the eye.

Sperm: The reproductive cells produced by the buck.

Standards: Normally up to 100 points, awarded to rabbits at shows. In Britain, Standards vary in points given to the special attributes of a new breed. Standards must be submitted to the Rabbit Council for scrutiny and approval before being accepted for the Official Standards Book.

Staple: The length of fur in Angora wool.

Stud: A collection of rabbits.

Stud buck: A buck used in mating.

Texture: Quality of the fur: the finer and silkier the fur the better in fur varieties.

Ticking: Hairs of a different colour to the main coat – shown by guard hairs only.

Tipping: The guard hairs.

Top colour: The colour furthest from the skin.

Tortoiseshell: Main colour is sandy yellow with black ticking.

Trimming: The removal of hairs, etc. to improve the look of the rabbit for show. A disqualification on the show bench and liable to severe penalty.

Type: The appearance and conformation of a rabbit.

Undercoat: The line of demarcation on the belly between the white saddle and hindquarters of a Dutch.

Undercolour: The colour from the base of the fur to the top colour in selfs and tan pattern varieties. In agouti or Chinchilla pattern, the colour to the pearling.

Wall eye: A blue eye of a different colour to the other eye, found in some Dutch and Chinchillas.

Wavy ticking: Ticking that has a waved appearance, as opposed to even ticking.

Weaning: The removal of youngsters from the doe.

Wool: A wool coat has no guard hairs. Angora is an example of such a coat. The presence of Angora bred into another, fur, breed becomes obvious when the fur is blown, for there is a tell-tale crimp at the base of the fur.

Woolliness: A type of fur showing the character of wool, which is a fault; breeders do not breed from them. A woolly rabbit is one without the top guard hairs.

World Rabbit Science Association: This association was modelled on the lines of the World Poultry Association and its beginnings date back to an international conference in Como, Italy in 1973. It took a further three years to become a reality, when representatives of several European countries, including Britain, worked out the constitution, which was finally adopted at Dijon, France in 1976.

Its main activity was the promotion of quadrennial conferences. The second one was held in Barcelona in 1980 and the third in Rome in 1984. These conferences lasted three to four days. Various scientific papers were presented on rabbit problems and the results of research into rabbit diseases, husbandry and nutrition, etc. The rabbit section no longer exists.

APPENDIX II

METRICATION TABLE

Simple conversion table of weights and measures.

250 grams	=	8 oz
500 grams	=	1 lb 1 oz
1 kilogram	=	2 lb 2 oz
1.5 kilogram	=	3 lb 3 oz
2 kilograms	=	4 lb 4 oz
5 kilograms	=	11 lb
6 kilograms	=	13 lb 2 oz
7 kilograms	=	15 lb 4 oz
10 millimetres	=	1 centimetre
2.5 centimetres	=	1 inch
5 centimetres	=	2 inches
15.2 centimetres	=	6 inches
30.4 centimetres	=	12 inches

NOTE: This book includes rabbits from many countries. Accordingly, there was difficulty in deciding whether to use Metric or Imperial measurements. Practical considerations dictated the use of both.

APPENDIX III
USEFUL
ADDRESSES

UK

British Rabbit Council (BRC)
Purefoy House
7 Kirkgate
Newark Notts
NG24 1AD

Telephone: (01636) 676042
Fax: (01636) 611683

Rabbit Welfare Association
PO Box 603
Horsham
West Sussex
RH13 5WL

Telephone: (0870) 0465249

Fur and Feather (the national rabbit magazine)
Mr & Mrs Gaskin
Printing for Pleasure
Elder House
Chattisham
Ipswich
Suffolk
England.

Telephone: (01473) 652789 or (01473) 652354
Fax: (01473) 652788

The Royal Society for the Prevention of Cruelty to Animals (RSPCA)

Wilberfore Way
Southwater
Horsham
West Sussex
RH13 9RS

Telephone: (0870) 0101181

The Scottish Society for the Prevention of Cruelty to Animals (SSPCA)

Braehead Mains
603 Queensferry Road
Edinburgh
Scotland
EH4 6EA

Telephone: (0131 339) 0222

This antiquarian bookseller sells books covering all small animals, poultry, pigeons, etc. and will send a complete list on demand:
Veronica Mayhew
Trewenna
Behoes Lane
Woodcote
Near Reading
RG8 0PP

Telephone: (01491) 680743

EUROPE

European Confederation of Rabbits, Pigeons and Poultry
A. Rudolph
General Secretary
Entente Européene D'Aviculture et de Cuniculture*
Altenhof 12
D-53804
MUCH
Germany

*Membership includes 20 countries.

USA

American House Rabbit Society
PO Box 1201
Alameda
CA 94501

American Rabbit Breeders Association (ARBA)
1007 Morrisey Drive
PO Box 426
Bloomington
Illinois, 61702